THE THINGS
OUR
FATHERS SAW

THE UNTOLD STORIES OF THE
WORLD WAR II GENERATION
FROM HOMETOWN, USA

Matthew A. Rozell

WOODCHUCK HOLLOW PRESS

Hartford · New York

Front Cover: "Stars over Berlin and Tokyo will soon replace these factory lights reflected in the noses of planes at Douglas Aircraft's Long Beach, Calif., plant. Women workers groom lines of transparent noses for deadly A-20 attack bombers." Alfred T. Palmer, Office for Emergency Management. Office of War Information. Public Domain Photographs, National Archives Number 535577, Unrestricted.

Back Cover: "Women workers install fixtures and assemblies to a tail fuselage section of a B-17 bomber at the Douglas Aircraft Company plant, Long Beach, Calif.". U.S. Office of War Information, 1944, public domain.

Any additional photographs and descriptions sourced at Wikimedia Commons within terms of use, unless otherwise noted.

Publisher's Cataloging-in-Publication Data

Names: Rozell, Matthew A., 1961- author.
Title: Homefront/women at war : the things our fathers saw : the untold stories of the World War II generation, volume IX / Matthew A. Rozell.
Description: Hartford, NY : Matthew A. Rozell, 2023. | Series: The things our fathers saw, vol. 9. | Also available in audiobook format.
Identifiers: LCCN pending | ISBN 978-1-948155-89-2 (hardcover) | ISBN 978-1-948155-40-3 (paperback) | ISBN 978-1-948155-76-2 (ebook)
Subjects: LCSH: World War, 1939-1945--Personal narratives, American. | Civilians--United States--Biography. |
www.matthewrozellbooks.com
www.teachinghistorymatters.com
Information at matthewrozellbooks.com.

Created in the United States of America

*~To the Memory of the Women
Of the World War II Generation~*

"There was one good thing came out of it. I remember going to [a] Sunday dinner one of the older women invited me to. She and her sister at the dinner table were talking about the best way to keep their drill sharp in the factory. I had never heard anything like this in my life. It was just marvelous! I was tickled."[1]

— Young Woman, Recalling Women Workers
During World War II

THE THINGS OUR FATHERS SAW IX:

HOMEFRONT/WOMEN AT WAR

THE STORYTELLERS (IN ORDER OF APPEARANCE):

HELEN QUIRINI

MABEL COLYER

FRANCES COOKE

ETHEL SEVERINGHAUS

RUTH A. BULL

LEONARD AMBORSKI

JANE WASHBURN

ELAINE CURREN SOMMO

SPENCER KULANI

KATHRYN GOODMAN FRENTZOS

KATHERINE G. DENEGAR

LILLIAN LORRAINE YONALLY

ROSE LANDSMAN MILLER

MARGARET DORIS ALUND-LEAR

HELEN MARCIL BRENNAN

KATHLEEN MARY DAVIE

JOYCE GRIFFIN

JOAN HOFFMAN

HALINA ROMAN

EVA KOENIG

LILY MULLER

THE THINGS OUR FATHERS SAW IX:

HOMEFRONT/WOMEN AT WAR

TABLE OF CONTENTS

General Electric's Fort Edward plant is the only completely government-financed factory in the Glens Falls area. A half of its workers live in Glens Falls.   Above, Jean Fitzgerald, Eleanor Penders, Phoebe Francato and Ruth Lopen test synchronous motors for automatic gun turrets on our largest bombers.

'General Electric's Fort Edward plant is the only completely government-financed factory in the Glens Falls area. A half of its workers live in Glens Falls. Above, Jean Fitzgerald, Eleanor Penders, Phoebe Francato and Ruth Lopen test synchronous motors for automatic gun turrets on our largest bombers.' LOOK Magazine, 1944.[1]

---

[1] Fort Edward High School's sports teams are still known as the "Flying Forts," after the Boeing B-17 Flying Fortress heavy bomber and the motors for the gun turrets built here.

Author's Note

The photograph on the facing page, a 1944 staged shot for a patriotic piece in a national news tabloid magazine showing young women employees of the General Electric plant—less than a five-minute walk from my childhood home—opens my first book in *The Things Our Fathers Saw*® series. Now returning nearly full circle, it is appropriate that I present it again here in the ninth volume, *Homefront/Women at War*.

This is one of the last, and one of the most difficult books in the series that I have undertaken, which was a bit unexpected when I began to lay it out. It turns out that many of the storytellers were relaying different versions of a similar story—that of being tasked with stepping up to answer their nation's call to fill the shoes of the boys and men called overseas, only to, when those veterans returned home, be expected to return to a form of second-class citizenship, in many cases giving up their newfound freedoms outside of the home, relegated to then wait decades for formal recognition from their country for their efforts.

My wife was reading a widely popular book series, which she enjoyed, but she noted that it seemed that every title carried the same plotline, but told it from a different perspective. So maybe something similar is going on with this book. Here is the perspective from the home front, featuring mostly women, from the eyewitness accounts of persons relatively ignored—over half the population.

I remember a quote from years past, which went something like, 'If it had not been for the women going out the door, there would have been no spring in 1944.' How very true.

Matthew Rozell
Labor Day, 2023
Washington County, NY

CHAPTER ONE

The Watershed

'The war changed my life completely; I found a freedom and an independence I had never known,' said one woman defense factory worker. Another recalled, [It] was the beginning of my emancipation as a woman. For the first time in my life, I found that I could do something with my hands besides bake a pie.'[2]

World War II was a watershed moment for the United States of America, and for the world. The America that emerged from the Great Depression and 'the War' would be in many ways almost unrecognizable. Yet when we think of the war today, how many of our countrymen stop to wonder how in the world we came together to fight the existential threat? And what about the seismic domestic change on the home front, in the absence of fathers, brothers, and sons? How did the lives of women change as they left the home, while still having to run the household?

Congressionally authorized conscription on a limited basis began in 1940 as war clouds darkened over Europe. After Pearl Harbor, the Selective Service had more than twelve million men in active service at its peak strength in 1945, with around sixteen million Americans serving in the military during World War II.[3] The economic and social effects and ramifications would be felt for generations as big government and big business worked hand in hand, and side by side with labor; even with postwar cuts, "the federal government in 1950 still had nearly twice as many civilian employees as it had in 1940, spent four times as much money, and had greater power."[4]

In July 1943, President Roosevelt said that, 'Every combat division, every naval task force, every squadron of fighting planes is dependent for its equipment and ammunition and fuel and food on the American people in civilian clothes in the offices and in the factories and on the farms at home.'[2] By 1944, a Liberty ship was made ready every two weeks. A B-24 Liberator heavy bomber rolled off the line every sixty-three minutes.[5] People moved from rural to urban areas in service to wartime industry or auxiliary assignment. Entire cities were created from nearly scratch, the Manhattan Project, which produced the atomic bomb, being the prime example. Oak Ridge, Tennessee, and Hanford, Washington, grew seemingly overnight where uranium and plutonium were extracted and processed by well over a hundred thousand workers; at Los Alamos, New Mexico, the bomb was developed and tested by legions of engineers and scientists with thousands of support staff. Dozens more related facilities rounded out the atomic effort.[6]

These massive production gains came at a high cost. Huge fractures in the tractional seams of American society were compounded on families already stressed by the absence of male members' military service. And what of the children? Many were left to grow up at a young age, unattended. Others were blessed with older sisters, who, though barely out of their own childhood years, assumed the duties of the frequently absent parents. Is it any wonder that some women never spoke of their wartime jobs?

---

[2] Franklin D. Roosevelt, "Fireside Chat," July 28, 1943.

School-aged children endured practicing drills, listening to frightening news reports dramatically broadcast over and over, hearing no word from brothers and fathers in uniform. It must have boosted anxiety levels sky high, although, comparatively speaking, American children were much better off than their counterparts in the overseas war zones. Imagine being a child refugee, watching as your younger siblings died, one after the other, *being on the run for an entire decade...*

*

Americans didn't physically suffer at home. They didn't starve, they were not subject to bombardment or invasion. The only continental US war dead directly due to enemy action on American soil came in May 1945 when a church youth group fell victim to a fluke small Japanese high-altitude balloon incendiary bomb in Oregon.[3] Americans flocked to the movies every week, listened to the radio, read their newspapers and comic books, enjoyed outings and other diversions. Still, nearly 185,000 American families didn't get to welcome a father, brother, or son back home, to say nothing of the psychological distress caused by the war. One girl remembered, 'Beginning on the first night Dad left, my mother had awakened me with her crying. I can remember going into her room and stroking her forehead while telling her everything would be all right, that Daddy would be home as soon as he could. I became what I was to remain for the rest of my mother's life—her daughter, her best friend and, in a sense, her mother.'[7]

Like the 'hard times' of the Great Depression in the preceding decade, this war affected every family. Few American communi-

---

[3] *The only continental U.S. war dead*-For further information, the reader may wish to visit www.history.com/news/japans-killer-wwii-balloons.

ties would remain unscathed by the emotional detritus of World War II.

PART ONE

WORKING

"We developed relationships with our co-workers, because if you have ever worked in any place for a long time, the people you work with are mostly people that you see every day. In fact, in a lot of cases, they're closer to you than your family. Of course, we all realized that when the guys came back, we would have to give up our jobs."

—Woman worker, General Electric Plant, Schenectady, New York

United States Office of War Information. Credit: George Roepp. Public Domain.

CHAPTER TWO

The Labor Activist

In the late 1800s, inventor Thomas Edison's business interests merged, with a main part forming the basis of the General Electric Works complex in Schenectady, New York, which would become one of the major industrial contributors to victory over the Axis powers on land, sea, and air.

For the Navy and the Merchant Marine, GE researchers, engineers, and workers created new types of propulsion systems that sped up ships and reduced fuel consumption; in fact, three-fourths of the World War II fleet's auxiliary turbine horsepower emanated from GE.

GE researchers had also developed early versions of radar, which would help Britain triumph in the Battle of Britain, and later, brought forth the radar jamming systems essential to Allied landing invasions. They also developed the autopilot systems and remote turret controls that increased the efficiency of air crews in the heavy bombers; by the end of the war, GE was producing the most essential components of the new B-29 Superfortress bomber, including power systems and heated flight suits necessary in the higher altitudes.

For land-based forces, this Schenectady plant also specialized in the construction of large motors for heavy vehicles and tanks. Smoke generators, lamps, lighting systems, and aerial searchlights were also a specialty. Because the rubber supply was strained by Japanese Pacific occupation, GE Schenectady developed high-performance polymers, molded plastics, and invented silicone.

X-ray technology was improved specifically to examine ordnance issues and determine if unexploded bombs were live. GE Schenectady also developed the appliances we take for granted today; advanced refrigerators, freezers, cooking ranges, and fire suppression systems aboard ships and in the field all improved the quality of life and hastened the end of the war in Allied victory. GE Schenectady was awarded the Navy 'E Ribbon' in 1942 and the Army-Navy 'E Ribbon' three times between 1942 and 1945.[8]

*

It may not have been glamorous work, but the men and women who labored here, epitomized by natural leaders like Helen Quirini, likely cut years off the war. Helen Quirini worked at the General Electric plant in Schenectady, New York, for thirty-nine years, beginning in April 1941, before Pearl Harbor, and retiring on her work anniversary in 1980. She followed her siblings into the war effort there but instead of an office job, she chose to work on the factory floor, due to its higher pay and her interest in saving for college. Instead, she became a pioneer of workers' and women's rights in the factory, the nascent union movement, and later, the national labor scene.

Helen Quirini

I was born on March 9, 1920, in Schenectady, New York. I had graduated high school and I started working at General Electric on April 1, 1941. I think Pearl Harbor happened after that. I worked in a factory. I did all kinds of jobs, assembling and wiring panels and little equipment needed for the war effort. I worked at General Electric for thirty-nine years. I started on April 1, 1941, and I ended on April 1, 1980. It was a great experience. I got active in my union because I fought this discrimination.

I [originally] didn't want to work at GE, for various reasons. My whole aim was to get enough money to go to college, [but for me], by the time the war was over, my father had died, so forget about college. But I was appalled about the bombings of England and knew that eventually, our country had to go to war. [At the time], my brother and I, we had started a grocery store [near the factory]. He went into the plant before I did because we were a little store, and we worked twelve hours a day, seven days a week. He went in, and then I went in. Of course, we developed relationships with our co-workers, because if you have ever worked in any place for a long time, the people you work with are mostly people that you see every day. In fact, in a lot of cases, they're closer to you than your family. When somebody died or something, we were there. When somebody had a child, we were there. When somebody was sick, we were there. It's something that today, they're not going to know, because what they say now, a person is going to work seven years or something, three or four jobs during their lives.

Pay Discrimination

When you first go into GE, you go on a training program, and they try to figure out where they can place you after the training program. I worked on some miscellaneous assembly and wiring, and then they moved you someplace else, which required a little bit more knowledge in reading blueprints and wiring diagrams, and handling a soldering iron and screwdrivers, and things like that.

I think [the pay] was two cents an hour, if I'm not mistaken. I think that was the minimum, and I am going to point out that women were paid less than men, which was shocking to me.[4] Also, males under the age of twenty-one were considered at the boys' rates. I used to go to [workers' lectures] during the Depression, and I'd meet young men, and I'd say, 'How come you're not working in GE?'

This was before the war, and they would say, 'We're too old.'

I said, 'What are you talking about?'

'We're over twenty-one and they're only hiring males under the age of twenty-one, so they can pay us boys' wages.'

We had three shifts, and we worked eight hours, but when the war started, we worked straight through for two weeks. They had to get special permission to let us work that long, but there were three different shifts, so we had to leave so the second shift could come in, and then the second shift had to leave for the third shift to come in. But there were times when we worked overtime, when the second-shift person didn't show up. But the regular hours, if I remember right, was the eight-hour shift plus overtime, and every Saturday and Sunday.

Wartime in the Factory

I was the chairperson to hold bond drives and blood donor drives and we had [bond] rallies. Three other women and I did that in our spare time. The company gave us that great big board, which is something like eight-by-sixteen. We had a crepe paper

---

[4] In 1940, the median pay for an American male worker was $956 annually. On average, an American woman earned 62% less than her male co-worker. Source: NPR, *The 1940 Census: 72-Year-Old Secrets Revealed*, April 2, 2012.

behind it, red, white, and blue. We had a cafeteria there and it was between the two doors in the cafeteria, and so it has a whole lot of things on it. There were also blood donor drives competitions throughout the whole plant. You can see on there if you read what the different areas were. And then, we also had little blood containers that were made into cardboard that we wore around our necks. So much for one pint, and so much for two, and so much for a gallon.

I used to write for the *General Electric Work News*, a history about what was happening there. We would put in who got married, who had a baby, who went to war, who came back to visit. And we had a fund, I think it was ten cents for each person a week; we gave to this fund, and if a service person ever came back [to work], we gave him ten dollars. But we had these rallies, especially to sell war bonds. During the rallies, we also talked about our co-workers [now overseas]. We were constantly reminded that we were at war, and we felt very deeply that we were important because without the materials that were created by the factories during this war, the war couldn't have been won.

We all had little badges in order to get into the factory, and there's that kind of security, and in order to get into certain rooms, you have to have had another badge, you know, so there was no doubt that we felt strongly about the war and cared about it very deeply because some of our people started losing their lives. In one of my articles I wrote for the news, I'm pleading for people to give blood and to buy bonds. Then I say something that, if you think you're making any sacrifice, look in front of the city hall, you will see sixteen thousand flags of the servicepeople from Schenectady, and if you look another place, you will see X number of flags for those who have already given their lives. So, it was a constant reminder of what had been happening. These friends of mine and I spent our time after work writing the names on those [displayed] nameplates and crosses. Those crosses have the names of the soldiers, the people who lost their lives. I think the big stars on nameplates are the names of the people who gave a gallon of blood, and the rest are the names of people in the services. And on top, it says, 'Lest we forget.' So, it was a constant reminder, if anybody had any doubts that we were at war or that we cared, this is a living proof of what has happened.

Recruiting Women Workers

Of course, everything was the way GE advertised it, [in recruiting women into their workforce]. We got wonderful restrooms and all this kind of junk, but anyway, that encouraged people to go in.

One of the articles [I worked on] said that some women [workers] were giving up their children because they could not find a place for them. So, I was now active with the union, and we got involved. During the war, there were special committees set up to talk about daycare. I mean, professional daycare, it is almost something that you don't even think about [today]. But, you know, when you read the article, [you learned that] women were giving up their children because they couldn't find a place and they had to work. And so, afterwards, I became president of a daycare center.

GE had classifications of men's and women's jobs. We, as women, could never even think about getting on a so-called man's job, and the differential in their rates was about three quarters. What GE used to do is, they'd set up a job description of what a job consists of, including safety and common knowledge and all that kind of stuff. And then when it went to a woman, they automatically cut it to three-quarters rate. So, most of us, not having the opportunity to work on so-called men's jobs, in most cases, we assumed they were very difficult. When the guys went to the service, and we went to work on those jobs, they weren't any more difficult than our jobs! Of course, the company always said, 'Well, it requires a lot of lifting,' but that was a lot of bull, because a lot of jobs don't require a lot of lifting! And so, we were kind of shocked. So, we worked on so-called men's jobs, and took the same skills that we had to do the little panels. In fact, the company, we used to have these, I think they were transmitters, and they used to be about that square [*gestures with hands*] and about six feet high, and so, you would wire everything in between. So then, the company got a great idea. They broke it down into little panels. They gave the women the little panels, and then they put connections between the panels so that they downgraded the man's job. I'm just trying to point out to you how much skill it took, but as a matter of fact, the skill was probably harder to do with the little panel [for women] because you didn't have that much room.

Of course, we all realized that when the guys came back, we would have to give up our jobs. One of the things that we had during some of this time, is the company had a double seniority list too. In other words, when the war was over, a man could bump a woman if he had less service. The whole country was in sort of a letdown in a sense because there were going to be a lot of layoffs when the men came back, and there were. And so, we had to fight all this kind of discrimination against women. Now, [don't forget], women were very tired because women in a lot of cases, they had to take care of the children and the houses, because you men did not do housework! It was beneath you! So, they had to do all this stuff. [A woman worker wrote in and] told about how she did her housework [and worked in the factory]. She was on second shift, she did her housework first, made do for the grandchildren, and she was very tired. She worked in a [position in] a place that was dirty, and GE—I don't know about today, but GE never had air conditioning in the plant. So, when it was hot, it was hot!

It didn't bother me that much, but I thought about the guys who worked in the foundry. I mean, they used to take their shirts off and work with no shirts on, because it was so hot. So, she's coming home, tired, and a couple of guys were talking about why the hell don't women stay at home and take care of their kids. She was so disgusted because, number one, she is trying to help out the war effort, and also to try to keep the family together. So, we had that fight! Of course, you get the idea, women's place is in the home and [they] used to say that we should be pregnant and bare-foot, you know. That was the feeling in those days in a lot of things. How would you guys like it if you went on a job and you were told, 'Well, you can't go on that at all, because of your sex?'

The Union

[In the beginning], I was against unions, because in the schools and in the newspapers, like a lot of the right-wing things are to-day, they're not very complimentary, especially in a place like Schenectady, where GE controlled everything. And so, my [first] ideas about unions were 'a bunch of Reds' and all this kind of stuff, and 'they take money away from you.' I had to do a lot of search-ing. My father hated unions, and my father worked three days for GE and quit. And so, I said to him one day, I said, 'How come you quit?'

He said, 'Don't be impertinent.'

In those days, you didn't talk back to your father, and so, he was mad because I got involved. He was mad because I went in the factory. My sister said to me when I came home, 'Let me see your hands.' She worked in the office. I've always worked around my house. I've always worked on my car. So, my hands were not any more calloused or swollen because I was working on jobs that required small tools. The thing is that I was on piecework, and when you're on piecework, you got to learn how to move, and you don't waste any time because you're getting paid by the piece.

Anyway, then I saw that discrimination; even when the first group came in, they had women leaders. I met with a very nice shop steward, and I said, 'How come you don't do anything?'

She said, 'Because nobody wants to put in a complaint.' And you have to have grievances.

So then, I got involved with a couple of other things; I went to a meeting. The woman there said, 'Any organization'—she wasn't just talking union—she said, 'Any organization, if you belong, take part in it. Make sure things are run right.' And if you look around at some of the things that are being done, in some of the organizations today, where the board of directors are not even doing what they're supposed to...

Then, I decided to go to another union meeting and sat and listened. The union was fighting some good cases about discrimination. They won a case with the War Labor Board, and the company stalled long enough, so when the war was over, they didn't put it into effect. So, having this kind of situation, I really got involved more with the 1946 strike, because I realized how important it was, and that I was going to be staying in GE, whether I liked it or not, because there were no jobs on the outside, you know, and where do you go without an education?

Now, during the war, our union was honored by the federal government and everything because of the great job that they did. While the war went on, the company got what you call 'cost plus.' Whatever they put in for a cost, they got a certain percentage above, so they were making money, not just them—I think the auto industry is the first one who started it. Through all of the country, the auto industry and everybody else was just reaping in money like mad. So, when we went in '46, we asked for some share of it, and they refused.

A labor historian interviewed Helen Quirini in 1993 where she recalled the 1946 strike, which was national in scope, as a turning point in her life, prolonged when the union refused to accept an inferior raise for woman members. "We stayed out for a couple of extra weeks, and I thought, 'Boy, isn't that great!' That... people were willing to sacrifice those weeks—and this is a lot of men, of course, mostly men!" [9]

I was active in the strike, with a lot of people, a lot of activities. Two of the same women who helped me with that were working in the factory, and we got tired of working the picket line. And so, we commandeered a beat-up truck that had a loudspeaker on top of it. Of course, if you know the General Electric plant, you have quite a few gates, and it was nine weeks in the winter. It was cold.

Anyway, we ran around with this truck, playing music, dancing with the guys. Lo and behold, when the thing was settled, there was an election for a secretary. I wasn't even running, and I was elected! I told the guys, 'I'm not qualified.' But when they took the job over, they weren't qualified either! I [filed] all the grievances for a couple of years. I worked that for two hours a day, I went in from seven to nine, and every grievance that was put in against the company, I recorded. Well, the guys before, they just put a couple notes on it, they had such scribbling! If a grievance went up to the next level, they would depend upon this paperwork for the business agent, to see what the arguments were. So, I brought in carbon paper, and I wrote in detail. I learned how to write nothing but the important things. And then, I put a copy of that in every grievance so that the business agent would have a copy. It wasn't just something [scribbled]. So, when I said I wasn't qualified, they said, 'Why do you demean yourself?' But that's how life is, you know? You can never understand how a woman feels being discriminated against the way we were, that you're not good enough to go on this job, you're not good enough to go on this job, and all that kind of stuff.

'We Felt the Danger to Our Country'

We had all kinds of rationing, you know, gas and butter and meat, and all that kind of stuff but, you know, this is a sacrifice. That's what's wrong with the [Iraq] war today, who the heck is sacrificing anything except the soldiers? We felt the danger to our country. As a matter of fact, and I'm speaking from memory, I think we were one of ten places in the country that if we're going to be bombed, we would be the place because of GE, the locomotive company, the Watervliet Arsenal, and the closest to the [state capital] at Albany. We had men and women standing on top of hilltops, watching for airplanes. All of the factory windows were blocked. We never saw the sunshine when we worked. There was a feeling of responsibility and even joy in being part of the sacrifice for something as important as that war. And as I say, that's what's wrong with this [current] war, who is sacrificing anything?

I remember, we laughed like mad because somebody said, 'Hey, I got some gas coupons, but you got to go to the certain garage.'

And so, if somebody went out a couple of miles to go there, spend all of his time with these [illicit] gas coupons, when he got there, he [would find] a gas lock on his tank.

I said, 'See, you're cheating, and that's what happens.'[Laughs]

But you got to remember that there was such a tremendous drive that people were bringing in their old furnaces, anything with steel. And if you went down some of the streets, you would see, there would be a big drive because the Japanese bought our steel from us, and then they made it into bullets and sent it back to us in that manner, for Pearl Harbor. So, we collected tin foil, grease, all that.

I'll talk a little bit about something that most people don't know about. There was an outfit called the block plan that was set up during the war. The block plan took every city. I'll just talk about Schenectady. It took Schenectady and it divided it down to blocks, but first, they divided down with, like, divisions. I headed a whole area, Mount Pleasant area, and each one, I had a block person in every block in that area. We used to have meetings once a month or even frequently, if there was news that had to be talked about the war. And if there was a push for blood, if there was a push for bonds, if there was a push for scraps, it was there. So, anything that could help, like the scraps that were so badly needed, we're constantly talking about it and talking about saving grease, and all this kind of stuff.

'I'm Doing a Good Job Where I Am'

I remember, one of the things I had done as chairperson, I brought in a recruiter. A very nice woman, looked very sharp. As she's talking about the need for people to sign up, somebody said, 'Helen, why don't you sign up [for the military]?'

And I said, 'Sure.'

She said, 'You know, you'd be a good candidate to go to office or school because of your experience. You're a shop steward, you know how to handle people, blah, blah, blah.'

She put her coat on me, and I must say, I looked pretty sharp. Then, I asked the sixty-four-dollar question.

I said, 'Let me ask you something. You're promising me that you're going to send me to the Paul Smith College or someplace, where my experience and my leadership and everything will be taken into consideration?

She said, 'I can't do that,' and I said, 'Forget it.' Because you know what happened? Some of our women joined up. They were doing a good job in the factory, and they ended up in the kitchen someplace. They wrote back and said, 'Helen, we're all sorry we signed up, because our skills were more needed where we were!'

As I say, they almost hooked me, but I figured, hey, I'm doing a good job where I am, because of the leadership that I showed about blood and bonds, and the *GE Work News*, which kept everybody connected. I was on a war production console during the war that was set up by the union and the company. We met regularly to talk about what can we do better in the shop to increase production. And so, I felt like I was doing my bit for the war effort.

You've got to remember that there were 40,000 people working at GE and women were thirty or thirty-five percent of them. We had a General Electric Athletic Association, and they had a tennis court, they had a ballpark, they had bowling alleys, they had places where you can play pool, they have places where you could meet and it was a great place for people to socialize. And so, and I was the only woman on that board, and so I worked hard too. I was a basketball player, I was a baseball player, I bowled, and so I worked very hard to let the women know that there was a place that was safe because some of the women came in from the [mountains and farms], and, I hate to say this, but boy, they had a ball taking these women out, you know, who were very inexperienced.

We stopped having some section nights for the union because it seemed like the guys—I don't want to be too derogatory, but you know what I'm saying—well, they had a ball with these young women. So, I finally got to the point where I told them, 'Look, you got all these women in the plant, you need a woman staff person' and they refuse to do it. I said, 'Look, I'm doing it already.' I'm working and trying to arrange all this stuff and put out publicity, but then they were too cheap to do that, so I resigned.

[When the men came back], we even had people come in from the federal government, the services, and we sponsored them. This one woman talked about syphilis, you know, I wrote an article for the *Work News* and they wouldn't put the word 'syphilis' in! 'Mrs. Kidman, you're going to talk about social diseases?' But one of the things that she said is very shocking because young men used to come home or come back from the service and have syphilis or something and they would say, 'Who were you with?' and the guy would say, 'We don't remember.'

'Oh, come on now. Who were you with? This person, if she gave that to you, is a danger.'

And so finally, they'd say, 'Well, you know, her name was Mary and she had blue eyes and I think it was in a section of Mount Pleasant.'

So, pretty soon, Mary got a knock on the door, 'We want to see you.' So this is some of the stuff that I did, you know. And that's why I felt like I was, in my estimation, more important here on the home front than if I had gone into the service. I know some of my friends joined the service and they were shocked. I mean, 'Geez, Helen, you were smart not to go in!'

*

You asked the question about the men's attitudes. Hey, the men have always resented women coming into the shop. Let's be honest. The attitude has changed lately, because of circumstances, but they have always resented the fact, I mean, you know, we used to stand in line at the clock and somebody would say something about, you know, 'Why don't you stay home and have a baby,' and I said, 'You know, guys,' I always had an answer for them.

I said, 'You know, get off of it,' and they'd laugh like mad because they knew that I always had an answer for them, you know, but they resented the fact that we were there. Let's be honest, though, regarding the amount of work that was after the Depression, if there had not been a war, there would have been a lot more people unemployed. But the fact is that one of the strengths that we had in Schenectady in the 1880s was led by women workers, but nobody knows about it because we have always been involved and the company used to say, 'Women work for pin money. Women can't lift, that's why they can't do jobs in the shop.' And the fact is that history has shown that 80% of the women who work support themselves and/or families, you know, so that knocked it off. We had to fight this whole thing about women.

Helen Quirini died on October 4, 2010, at the age of 90 after years of service to GE workers and retirees, a pioneering voice for women.

Shift Work Sisters

The Long sisters of central New York, like many young women, played a critical role in supporting the nation's war effort by working a major defense plant in Sidney, New York, during World War II. Frances was born December 30, 1916, in Syracuse; her sister Ethel followed on December 10, 1918, and Mabel came along on April 3, 1921. They sat for this interview with the New York State Military Museum in 2003.

Mabel Colyer

Frances Cooke

Ethel Severinghaus

Ethel: We worked in the same defense plant, the Bendix Scintilla Airplane Magneto Plant in Sidney, New York, [supplying the starting engines for the US Navy planes].[5] It went from that, to Bendix, to another name before Amphenol, which it is now.

---

[5] During World War II, the company was a major manufacturer of magnetos used on American aircraft engines.

Mabel: They still make connectors and stuff for planes, although they make more domestic products now. In fact, back then, it was the only decent employer in the whole area. People would come in from Pennsylvania and everywhere to work there. It still is, really.

Ethel: The railroad brought people from Middletown, to Edmiston, to Sidney for work. The train had three shifts, it would bring a group and then go right back and get another group. I was there briefly, just several months, between one thing and another. I was in the inspection, inspecting cams and a few other things they dragged me into. We had no experience, except my sister had been in inspection for a long time. I knew a little bit about it from her. I was there from September to December, 1941.

Frances: I was there from the fall of 1936 to the fall of '44. I worked on Rockwell machines, which had a diamond point and an indicator you pressed down to metals to find out if they were the correct hardness that was needed. I also worked on the springs, which were very important, used in cam followers; they were little pieces of felt fastened to a spring and the spring had to be tested 100% for each piece, because it was very important. They were used in the airplanes. I also worked with other things, like cable screws and stuff they used in the molding room. I am trying to think of what else.

Mabel: I worked there from 1940 until 1945 when the war was over. I worked on the magneto spark plug assemblies, and it was mostly just general assembly work. They all went into the ignition system for airplanes. It was mostly all airplanes, magnetos, and assemblies. We really don't know whether they made as many during the war as before, but they were building all these extra planes and everything. It was Scintilla Magneto, originally started by German immigrants, and they, by the way I was told, made just about all the magnetos that were used on the planes at that time.

There was no country or place that made them more than they did, Scintilla, in Sidney. But we really don't know who did it, if it was men, before we went there, because there were just more women and they had to split mica, and make the center core of the spark plugs, and assemble them. At that time, you did one or two jobs and that was it. That's the way they made production.

Frances: [Being there well before the war], I'd say [the sex ratio of the workers was] half and half.

'You're More Talented Than That'

Interviewer: Why did the three of you end up there?

Frances: I started out to be a nurse, and my father kept complaining that he wanted me home helping him. I got so tired of his complaining that I told him I guess I would stop my nursing for a while. I went there and my Aunt Louise said to me, 'Well, Frances, you shouldn't just work in my store. You're more talented than that. Why don't you go down and apply to the plant?'

They told me they wouldn't hire me for quite a long time, but the next morning, I got a call to come in.

I said, 'Well, why would you hire me?'

They said, 'Because you had physics and chemistry in high school.' They figured that would go along with their metals.

Interviewer: What kind of shifts did you work, did you work a swing shift?

Frances: I worked the day shift, but during the war, I worked from 11-7, nights, and sometimes the next day shift. Sometimes I was working sixteen hours a day.

Mabel: The war was on by then, we worked ten hours a day, seven days a week. The only time you saw daylight was if you went outdoors at your lunchtime, because the windows were all blacked over. I lived in Oneonta at the time, and they used everything that moved on the road to get people back and forth to work. I remember the old bus which had school seats like they had in old schools, bolted to the floor. That's what we rode. A lot of people from other towns took the train, any way they could get to Sidney, because Sidney was the only defense place in the area.

Mabel: The plant was secured by the military with a fence all around. There were guards, they had Army and Navy personnel in the plant to make sure that quality control was kept the way it had to be, and things like that.

Ethel: Well, [for me] it was a day shift because I had to go down with the riders from Sidney Center. I was a schoolteacher, and I was really working during the four months between my summer work and marriage. I was married in December, and of course, the war was declared three weeks before I was married. I had to move to Saranac Lake where my husband was a regional game supervisor.

Thirty Cents An Hour

Frances: We were paid thirty cents to start out with and I ended up with a dollar and a quarter when I quit.

Mabel: I don't really remember what my early wage was.

Frances: At Christmastime they gave us a little piece of ham.

Mabel: The only thing we got was extra stamps for gas, but then everybody carpooled. And of course, as I said, we rode on the bus. At the time, my husband was in the National Guard, and he was down in Alabama, Fort McClellan. Everybody from Oneonta got to the plant any way they could. It was mostly carpooling and these old buses. They would put anything on the road that traveled and could take people to work. Anybody driving in carpools got some extra stamps for gas if they took passengers.

Frances: They pushed a lot of war bonds, they had to ask us to buy them. We were supposed to buy a $25 one every month. We got a $25 bond for $18.75. With our small pay, you can see how much we gave up.

Mabel: When the war ended, we had a celebration, everyone went crazy. We were laid off, they closed the plant right down, and everybody went home. About a week later, if they wanted you to come back, you got a letter. I received a letter, but I didn't go back until five years later, and then I put in another twenty-one years there.

Ethel: We were very conscious on the job because we knew those planes were dependent on our doing our job properly. At one time, a fellow who had been an upperclassman when I was in college crashed in a plane in the Pacific and died while I was working there.

Mabel: Everybody was working long hours, but we took it in stride because we had a good purpose for doing it. It wasn't like we were working long hours for somebody else's profit. We were doing it because of the war effort. That's all you did, went to work and came home. We felt quite proud of the work we were doing; it was worth it.

The Long sisters lived rich, full lives into the 2010s, with the oldest, Frances, passing at age 102.

CHAPTER FOUR

The Los Alamos Secretary

Ruth Bull graduated from Schenectady High School in 1938 and soon after, she was employed as a secretary at General Electric in Schenectady and worked on the Manhattan Project in Los Alamos, New Mexico, during World War II, with an eyewitness view to the goings-on surrounding one of the most important projects in history.

Ruth A. Bull

I was born in Rotterdam, New York, on February 7, 1920. I finished high school, in a commercial course [with secretarial training].

I remember about Pearl Harbor that it was on Sunday, and I was working down at General Electric at that time. That day, I was home and getting ready to go out for the day, but instead we stayed home and listened to the radio. Well, it felt so sad, so bad. Didn't know what was going to happen next. That's what was so bad. And the next day, of course, going to work on Monday, and it was talk about what was going to happen.

Interviewer: How long did you stay at GE?

I was there from 1940 to 1945, doing secretarial work. I ended up with the Los Alamos Project when my sister and my brother-in-law were called. He was a glassblower at GE, and he was personally asked to go to Los Alamos. And so, he went, and my sister went with him. I said to her, 'Well, I'd like to come out. Maybe I could be your maid. I'd like to see what New Mexico looks like.'

And so she turned my name into personnel, and then they sent me an application and information about going, so I applied; my fare was paid by the government. And that's how I got out there, to be a secretary; we didn't have to have any specific training, but you couldn't leave the Hill. They called it the Hill. It was 2,000 feet above sea level and then it was like a mesa up there. [There was a lot of security around it]; you couldn't get in or out without identification. And you had to sign in the time you left and the time you came back.

I enjoyed my work there. I lived in a dormitory, with about twenty people in each dorm. They were all men and women. My sister lived in a house, apartment, or duplex house. We were well supplied with food. We didn't have to worry about any food. They had a commissary, and you were able to buy your own. They also had a mess hall facility.

Were there any special precautions you had to take with the kind of work you did at all?

No, not at that time. We handled some things that were contaminated; you had to be careful what you handled and to know how you had to handle it, get it out of the office fast and do not handle it too much. I had a Geiger counter on my desk. And if it flipped, well, then you had something in there that was contaminated, and you had to get it out of there. Get it moving.

We worked a full eight hours and sometimes more, depending on what job had to be done. You couldn't say anything about where you worked, how you worked, or what you did. It wasn't much for me, but I worked in an office. The military took care of the civilians. There were three or four people that worked in our office who were civilians. After I got there, there were more people that were hired civilians in our office, but we had a couple. I know that one of my best friends was in the Army. She was in charge of radiation reports. She had to be locked in when she was doing those reports. We were all combined all the while. At the door, we had about four MPs because you couldn't go in and out of the building unless you identified yourself with a pass, in every building.

Dr. Fermi and Dr. Teller

I met [the scientists], Dr. Fermi and Dr. Teller, they all worked in the technical area. We all worked in the same area. They were nice, especially Dr. Fermi. He was my favorite. Everybody looked the same. The only one you could tell was different was Teller. Do you know Dr. Teller? I didn't [really] like him, he was so boisterous. There were dances. We had dances on weekends; not every weekend, but once in a while. Dr. Fermi liked to do square dancing with me. His wife did not dance, she didn't want to square dance. So he picked me. It was fun. Everybody was very friendly. I only saw Robert Oppenheimer a few times. Half the time he was incognito; he was working all the time or somewhere else, he was always on the move.

The [scientists] lived in private homes. Originally, it was a private school. That's where Oppenheimer went to school as a child. They had a few homes that were very well-built—stone and brick. He lived in one of those, not too far away, all the dorms and everything were built around it. It was a very small area.

We had quite a few movies in one building. We had church there, too. Just entertaining. I met a lot of my sister's friends that were married people. I spent a lot of time with them. I had dinners with them, and we played cards a lot. But then, after the drop of the bomb, they were more liberal. Some of the GIs were able to bring their wives up on the Hill.

'As If It Was Noontime'

Do you have any memorable events that you think stood out more than others while you were there?

The night before the first test of the bomb. I mean, they had several different tests down in the southern part of New Mexico. We would hear about them being duds or not or about them being successful. But the night that the big one was going to be dropped, it was a sort of funny feeling because you got the feeling that you didn't know whether it was going to be successful or not. And they were worried. They were worried, because they didn't know whether it was going to start a chain reaction and start the world on fire. They were pretty sure of what was going to happen, but they weren't positive, so we stayed up all night waiting for that first test. And it happened at 5:30 a.m. We were 250 miles away from it, but it was as if it was noontime. But everybody that went down to see the test, to be there, all had to have permission to go. My boss went. And they couldn't watch it anyway because they had to turn away from it and they had to wear special glasses.

They couldn't look toward it at all. And so we saw more of the fire and the color and it was just like fire. And it just kept rolling and rolling. It was so bright. It wasn't close, but you could hear the rumble at 250 miles. And see, that was the southern part of New Mexico, and we were in the north, so the sound rose higher and came up high.

This is what the bomb did, it turned the sand to glass. This is kind of crude, but some of it was beautiful. The colors in it were really nice. I had a pail of it. My boss brought up a pail. And so, then we had this GI, anyway, he worked in the department where he could put it in plastic. He made bookends and different things like this for everybody to have a piece to take home.

Why didn't you let the family look at this for a long time?

Because it was contaminated. It isn't too big a piece, but it was radioactive.

Home

From there, I went to Columbia University. The professor I had in our department was Dr. Mitchell from Columbia. He was a physicist. He was the head of our department. And so, I followed him to New York, and I worked at Columbia University in the government contracts office at the time. And then I didn't stay there very long, and then I worked in... I ended up working in the alumni house, and then after that I had to come home because my twin sister was supporting my mother. Well, I was too, but indirectly. Finally, I did come back home.

I came home in 1946. My sister and her husband went directly to Oak Ridge, Tennessee, and continued to work with atomic energy, for twenty years or more, until he retired.

'Never Questioned Me About the Bomb'

I was still in contact with one engineer friend that I had that was in the Army, and we still write Christmas cards. And another girl that moved up to Seattle, I kept in contact with her for many years. I have a certificate for working on the Manhattan Project, and the pin was also issued to each one of us, signed by the Secretary of War, Mr. Stimson, a kind of [token] that at least we did something for the war effort.

What was your reaction when you heard about the atomic bombs being dropped on Japan?

Terrible. Also, we had to go to a couple of lectures because of it being dropped on so many women and children. It was so bad, so that we didn't... At first, I didn't know what they meant, what they were [having us be briefed for]; why? But afterward, I thought about it. Because after you start thinking about it, you think how terrible it was. It was so that we didn't feel so guilty. But, we did. We had those lectures afterward. Since then, though, we went to a talk about Los Alamos, just a few years ago, and one man came up to me after we talked about how I got there. He said, 'I want to thank you for working on that atomic bomb.'

I said, 'Oh, gee, thanks.' And he noticed my pin.

I said, 'That's the first time that anybody's ever said anything to me.' That's when I quit feeling guilty. You can't help thinking of it all these years.

He said, 'You saved many, many more people than were killed by that bomb.' And it's true. And we were good friends with a Japanese girl, after the war. But she never questioned me either, did she? Never questioned me about the atomic bomb.

Ruth Ann Bull passed on February 10, 2008, at the age of 88.

CHAPTER FIVE

The Research Physicist

Leonard Amborski was a civilian teaching physics when he was called upon to go to Washington, DC, working on new secret magnetic compasses for the military, to gear up for the anticipated invasion of Japan. He gave this interview in 2008 at the age of 86.

Leonard Amborski

I was born on August 23, 1921, Buffalo, New York.

I was at my date's house on a Sunday afternoon, we had the radio on and we got the message about Pearl Harbor then. I never heard about Pearl Harbor until then, didn't know where it was. Most people didn't. It didn't take long to find out what happened and so on, further comments on the radio filled us in on the details.

I was still a student at Canisius College. I graduated March 1943 and started teaching Army Air Corps cadets who were stationed at the college. They had just started the program, the college training detachment, at that time so I taught them physics and I also taught the civilian classes in physics at Canisius starting in

May 1943. The Air Corps students had just arrived that month, there were two hundred of them in the original group. They were taking a five-month course, four months were classwork and one month they spent learning how to fly. We taught them pertinent physics subjects that might be important for them to know as fly-ers in combat.

We designed the course. We selected the parts that we thought were important for them to know. We tried to teach them some of the mechanics of airplanes, why they fly, the Bernoulli Princi-ple, what kept the plane up in the air.[6] We taught them things on computers, computing distances and time so they would have some idea of instrumentation. We taught them things like elec-tricity, a little bit of meteorology, too.

'Not Allowed to Discuss the Nature of Our Work'

In May 1944 they were ending the college training detachment program for the Army Air Corps. At that time, they had a need for scientists at the Department of Terrestrial Magnetism, which is the Carnegie Institute in Washington. There were eight of us on the faculty who went to Washington, D.C. to work at the Carne-gie Institute. We were assigned to various activities; I was doing work on magnetism, studying the magnetic effects of the earth. I also worked on magnetic compasses and compasses for the Air Force, the Navy, and Coast Guard. Of those eight people, many of them were sent overseas because we were compiling data on the

---

[6] *Bernoulli Principle*- 1738 theory of flight that states "an increase in the speed of a fluid occurs simultaneously with a decrease in pressure or a de-crease in the fluid's potential energy" and is to calculate the lift force on an airfoil. Source: www.skybrary.aero/articles/bernoullis-principle.

ionosphere, which is related to radio transmission. People were sent as far as Baffin Bay, Alaska, Christmas Island, Trinidad, and they were at these stations where we were compiling magnetic data as well as ionospheric data. Fortunately, I happened to be staying in Washington where I worked on the compass work and also on detecting and deactivating mines. We were anticipating an invasion of Japan at that time so they brought in a lot of Japanese mines and we were doing research on how to deactivate these particular mines to protect our troops if they were going to invade Japan.

We designed compasses specifically, one of the most detailed ones was for the Air Corps. These compasses were designed to make sure pilots would get to their destination and get back. We also were designing compasses for the Coast Guard and were actually on a Coast Guard ship in Glen Burnie near Baltimore where we were testing these compasses. They were automated and they would be recording the data as you went along. Rather than just looking at a compass, they would have recording devices, the early stages of computerization.

We worked five and a half days, Monday through Friday and then half a day on Saturday. It was a beautiful setting in Rock Creek Park. The buildings I worked in primarily were non-magnetic buildings because we didn't want the outside influence of the building having any steel or magnetic material. The building that I worked in was a rather unique building in that it was all wood and they used copper nails to put it together. We studied compass deviations and how they might be affected by the outside influences.

We were essentially qualified [with a high security clearance] by the War Manpower Commission. They looked at our credentials in terms of training and knowledge and experience, so they gave us an exemption from being military people. At one time they considered putting us into the military, but they said what's the point, we're doing the same work anyhow, so the War Manpower Commission kept us as civilians. We were not allowed to discuss the nature of our work.

I worked in Rock Creek Park, which was northwest Washington, but I lived right across the street from the US Capitol building. I got married when I was there and we lived in an apartment directly across the street. If you were in our bathroom, you could look out the window and see the dome of the Capitol. *[Laughs]* We didn't have a car, we used public transportation. For $1.25 we had a pass, you could go anywhere in the city on a trolley or a bus. I also taught night school there; I taught chemistry in one of the public high schools, Theodore Roosevelt High School, but I lived at the other end of town. We had a lot of exciting days because we lived right across from the Capitol and any dignitaries coming in, we'd get a chance to see them. One of the most notable things I remember is seeing President Roosevelt the day he left the White House to go to Warm Springs, Georgia, before he died. He was in an open car with his fedora and I took a picture of him. That was the last time I saw President Roosevelt. To me he was a hero. I felt very badly about that.

On the way to work one day, I met, coming out of the apartment building, on Connecticut Avenue, President Truman, the day he took over the office. He lived in an apartment; I saw him come out of his building that morning after Roosevelt died. I also remember seeing General Charles de Gaulle, he was on the street one day. Those are the two dignitaries other than Eisenhower and Wainwright whom I saw in parades. But I got pretty close to President Truman at the time and de Gaulle.

We also enjoyed the parades they had when Eisenhower came to Washington and General Wainwright, there was great celebration. We also had a daughter born that year, and when the Japanese war ended in August 1945 my wife and I were pushing the baby carriage down Pennsylvania Avenue rejoicing with everybody else. My two-month-old daughter was sound asleep in the carriage, she didn't hear anything.

We knew nothing about [the dropping of the atomic bombs]. When it happened, having been alerted to the possibility that we might have to invade Japan, knowing the consequences of our people being killed, I was very happy to see that we saved a lot of our own lives. Probably tens of thousands of American lives were saved as a result.

[Rationing was a part of our lives], definitely. My wife used to go to the local store, and he'd give her a package. You didn't know what it was you came home with, probably hamburger so you never knew what you got. Butter and meat were very scarce, hard to come by. We had a lot of Spam. [Laughs] My wife was pregnant, so we did a lot of walking, a lot of sightseeing. We got to see many things in Washington, Glen Echo Park, we went to the Franciscan Monastery, so we got around the town to see what was there. Of course the Lincoln Memorial, we walked around the Tidal Basin, we always enjoyed the cherry blossoms there. So we did a lot of sightseeing around the town, that was our major effort. I don't think we even went to movies in those days, we just did sightseeing.

'I Lost Two Brothers'

My brother and I started school together at Cleveland and went through every class together through freshman year at Canisius College. He was eleven months older than I was, so we were almost like twins. He spent one year at Canisius and then went in the Coast Guard and ultimately went to the Merchant Marine

Academy on Long Island. Part of their training was to be on a merchant vessel. He was assigned to a merchant vessel which went to England. On the way back they were torpedoed and that's where he lost his life. I spent four years researching this in recent years and published a book.[7] That was the most tragic event in my life. I still recall my mother when she screamed when she got the message. All we learned at that time was that he was missing in action. It wasn't until about three months later that my mother got a letter from the mother of one of the survivors of the ship, giving us the details of how it happened. My mother was in a bad state of mind for a long time after that. It did affect the family very strongly. My father kept writing letters trying to find out more information. I still have copies. It was a real tragic event for the whole family.

I also lost a cousin, Arthur Amborski, whose mother and my mother were sisters and our fathers were brothers. They were married in a double wedding. He was like a brother to me. He went to Bergen High School, he was a four-star athlete, he was in football and basketball, he was class president, he was an honor student. He had an offer to play professional baseball with the Cleveland Indians but when he graduated in 1943, he joined the Air Force and ultimately wound up in Italy and he was a gunner on a plane.

They were shot down over Vienna, Austria, and he was killed. He was buried in a cemetery in Austria and four or five years later they exhumed his body and he's now buried in Ardennes, Belgium. So I basically lost two brothers in the war.

After the war I joined DuPont where I worked forty-four years. During the course of my career at DuPont I went to night school at the University of Buffalo and got my Master's and PhD at night

---

[7] *The Last Voyage: Maritime Heroes of WWII.*

school. I was the first student to do that. I got my PhD in chemistry and worked for DuPont in research and I got to do environmental work. I got to do fitness work and got to be an industrial hygienist. I had to take a training program and pass a certification exam and I was the first certified hygienist in western New York. That entailed my efforts to look after the health of our workers. We tested the area for toxic material, noise, radiation, stress, mechanical stress. I got to be an industrial hygienist as well as a research chemist. It's just an inherent interest I had in research, I still have that same interest. Now I do my research in genealogy. I'm still researching all the time, I guess that's my nature. I started out that way and I maintained that same interest in looking into new things. *[Laughs]*

Leonard Amborski passed away on January 8, 2014 at the age of 92.

PART TWO

HOME & SCHOOL

"The servicemen, most of it was just party time, really. Servicemen came in and all they wanted to do is eat, sleep, and drink, they figured this was their last chance. They would have a big party and they figured if they left Hawaii, they would be dead, so all they wanted to do was party. A lot of them did not even come back."

—School kid remarking about his family's restaurant, Pearl City, Hawaii

CHAPTER SIX

The School Teacher

Jane W. Washburn was born a week before the Armistice ceasing the hostilities of the 'Great War' was signed in 1917. She grew up on a farm during the Depression in Gansevoort, New York, and graduated from Glens Falls High school in 1935. Unlike many in her generation, she went on to graduate from a private college in 1939, earning a degree in home economics, remembered by her students for holding high standards in her classroom. She gave this interview to a pair of my high school seniors in 2003, having enjoyed many days of travel in her retirement. On one of her many travels, she visited Japan; she was very impressed with their lifestyles and friendliness, but, as she stated, her 'old feelings towards them still remained.' Here, she offers her insights into growing up in 'Hometown, USA' as the Great Depression and World War II and its aftermath unfolded.

Jane Washburn

I was born on this property and my grandfather was four years old when he came here to live back in 1854. He came, so the Washburns have lived here all this time. How I feel about the wars and the Depression are somewhat colored by my family's background for generations, if you know what I mean.

I was born before the Armistice. Therefore WWI, WWII, Korean War, Vietnam War, Palestine, and Israel, Wars in Africa, Gulf War, and the present two wars have all been a part of my life. I have had very few years in my life when there's been total peace in the world. Too bad, isn't it? *[Pauses]* Now you want to know about the Depression?

Depression Days

The big crash came in 1929. I was a teenager, of course, during the Depression. Nobody had any money, anyway. At first, I went to a little private school, then I went to school in South Glens Falls. I took the trolley! I had to walk up the road here and took the trolley from there, from South Glens Falls. At the end of seventh grade, I was sent to the Glens Falls High School because it had a better curriculum. My parents, neither one of them had education beyond high school; they wanted it for their three daughters. So, my sisters and I, all of us graduated from the Glens Falls High School. My family paid tuition for that. So we didn't have any money, but living on a farm made a difference.

We always had plenty of food. Plenty of milk, plenty of eggs, plenty of butter, plenty of meat, lots of vegetables. If you wonder what might have contributed to the fact that today I'm 86 and still navigating, it might be because I had a long walk every day to catch the bus. We got plenty of exercise; we didn't have time for a lot of foolishness. *[Laughs]* We took piano lessons, you know, and all of those things.

My older sister graduated two years ahead of me and went to Russell Sage [College]. So when it was time for me to go to college and I was interested in home economics, Russell Sage was the place. They had a very good economics department there then. My sister graduated two years ahead of me. It was Depression days, but we each got an allowance of four dollars a month. A dollar a week! How would you like that? *[Laughs]*

Miss Jane Washburn, 1939. Source: Jane Washburn.

In fact, I was a sophomore in college before we got electricity. One of the biggest things that Franklin D. Roosevelt did as President was to bring about rural electrification. It was a wonderful, wonderful thing to be able to flip a switch and have a light. This is digressing, but my mother and father heard about this, you know. So-and-so out in such-and-such a place is getting electricity. My mother said, 'Why don't we have electricity?' So, she called Niagara Mohawk [Power Company] and they said, 'If you want electricity, you get all the people in the community together that want it and I will come and tell you about it.' So everybody called everybody, and they all met down there at the farmhouse and had a big meeting. One month later, they had electricity, it was just wonderful!

We didn't have a lot of clothes. We didn't have cars, but we did have a very good education. I graduated in 1939 and it was right around the time when schools were beginning to centralize. With centralization, they put in a lot of new departments. Home Economics was one, agricultural courses was another, industrial arts courses, all things that were going to be helpful to train people in the Depression days.

So I went out to western New York to teach for 1,200 dollars a year. Worked ina school that had no economics department, nothing, but I got it going. I was there for six or seven years, and I was there during Pearl Harbor.

I didn't know anything about it until that night. [*Pauses*] When I heard, somebody had the radio on. This was in [Ripley], New York. That's the last town left of New York State, it's right on the Pennsylvania border. My sister was teaching at Newfield, which was just south of Ithaca. She taught French! Somebody always had a radio on. When they heard a piece of news, they immediately got onto the telephone and then that person got the radio on. This is how news got around, and that's how I got the news. Somebody had the radio on and heard about Pearl Harbor. As I told you before, I was indignant because I had been to the movies previous to this and knew that two ambassadors from Japan had come to visit Franklin Roosevelt at the White House, the day before the seventh.[8] They never let on that all of this was being planned, you see. We all knew that something was going on; we didn't know what it was.

'Nobody Really Knew'

As I told you I think previously too, my roommate's boyfriend joined the [Army] Air Force in the summer of 1940, and he was a pilot on the B-17s. He flew to Manila, the plane had all the armaments it needed, but it had no ammunition. He was there when Clark Field was bombed. The only thing he saved was his camera. Then he had a hard time getting out. It took months to get out of the Philippines, you see, all this time the war with Europe was going on too. Here again, if you wanted to know something, you had to go to the movies. To see the Pathé newsreels they used, to see about the battles and things and whatnot. There was lots of talk about what Hitler was doing, but nobody really knew. The terrible things, we had rumors of it, but nobody really saw it. No one ever knew! Then when Pearl Harbor came, all the Japanese [-American] people were rounded up. You've probably seen pictures of that, haven't you? They had prisoner of war places for them. Many innocent people were [rounded up]. People of foreign descent! [A friend] who was up here on Mount McGregor, she'd been there for 20 years, a Japanese girl, but after that she was

---

[8] *two ambassadors from Japan-* Secretary of State Cordell Hull met with the diplomats at 2:20 pm, Washington time, on December 7, where they were to deliver the message that the Japanese government was formally breaking off relations with the United States. Unbeknownst to the officials, the Japanese had commenced their attacks. Hull, now aware of the perfidy, lectured them and dismissed them after ten minutes.

temporarily relieved of her job as caretaker up there.[9] We had German people, we had Austrian people and we were very suspicious, we couldn't help it.

Rationing

It was really after Pearl Harbor that things began to tighten up. You couldn't buy an automobile, you couldn't buy tires, and gasoline was rationed. Here on the farm, of course, we were able to get more gasoline, because we didn't live in town.

Now to get back to after Pearl Harbor, we began to have rationing; sugar was one of the first things to go, butter was another. We had olio, which was just the color of Crisco, you know. You had to put colored things in it to perk it up. Meat was terrible, Spam, I can't eat it even today. Hot dogs you could get, they were the mixtures of things. We had lots of vegetables; we had our own pork. Now and then we would have a piece of beef. We had a dairy farm, so that's why we had beef. In the town where I was teaching, they got the rationing. The teachers were one group of people that could always get together to get a job done, so the teachers were responsible for signing all the people in that town

---

[9] *Mt. McGregor*-Mt. McGregor, located in Wilton, New York, about 10 miles south of Glens Falls, has an interesting history. Originally settled by Native American survivors escaping King Philip's War, it boasts spectacular views. Duncan McGregor built a hotel called the Mountain House in 1876; in 1885, the new owner, Joseph Drexel, loaned the use of his personal cottage on the mountain to his friend, then seriously ill former president Ulysses S. Grant, where Grant finished writing his war memoirs in just six weeks before he died there that July. Today, the Grant Cottage State Historic Site is preserved exactly as it was at the time of his death. In 1945, New York State used it for convalescing WWII veterans, and from 1976-2014 it was used as a minimum-security state prison.

up for rationing. You got stamps for gasoline and for butter, and for various foods. Canned foods and meat and meat products, you see. This is beside the point, but we had one famous person in this little town. He was a Civil War veteran, and he was one of the last ones to die. He was over a hundred years old when he died, but he was a vegetarian. So anyway he was very, very patriotic. So when rationing came along in that little town, everybody who had any extra stamps or canned vegetables or canned fruits, they gave to the grocer for Grandpa Rounds when he did his shopping. But Grandpa Rounds would never ever give anybody one of his meat stamps, because he thought it unpatriotic. Yet, he never knew that everybody in that town was keeping him well fed with their extra stamps. We all knew! [Laughs] He was rather interesting!

Paper Salvage scrap drive: "A young woman, Jean F. Casey, staffs a booth on Glen Street, Glens Falls. Sign reads, 'WANTED 250 MEN to help win the war.' Banner below her reads in yellow, 'It is a weapon of war,' and in white, 'SAVE WASTE PAPER.'" Source: LOOK Magazine for 'Hometown USA' series, 1943-44. The Folklife Center at Crandall Public Library, Glens Falls, NY.

We all got along somehow or another with what we had. We had lines that would form! If you were walking along Glen Street in Glens Falls, and you saw a line, you would know someone had cigarettes or they had candy or some little thing. You would get into line, whether you would want it or not. Buy the product, maybe for somebody else who did want it and couldn't get there, you know.

Stockings, we got so we couldn't get nylon stockings. We had to wear rayon stockings, which would run. It was weak when it was wet, so you would get runs in them all over. We had to wear cotton stockings but somehow, we managed to do that, too.

Travel was very hard! I sat on my suitcase from west of Buffalo to Albany on the train one day. Now that's a long time, it's about six hours. I had to sit in the aisle on my suitcase because there were no seats on the train, you see. The train, well there would always be men on the train, servicemen on the train. That was the first time I think when gentlemen did not have to give up their seats to a lady! If you saw a serviceman on, he got to sit. I took a trip on an airplane and if you were changing planes in like Chicago and there was a serviceman waiting to get on that plane, he got on, you were bumped. They had priority, which was probably right because many of them were tired and many of them didn't know where they were going or what their futures were going to be. In 1945, I went to Galveston, Texas, to see this college roommate of mine who had a new baby. Her husband had come home and was flying out of the airbase there, he was a weather expert. I got bumped every stop from Buffalo, then Detroit, then I think it was Chicago and Kansas City and Dallas, Texas. It took me 24 hours to get there, which now you would do in about 4-6 hours. Then the planes were not big planes like they are today, of course.

There were a lot of recipes by the way, too, for egg-less cakes and butter-less cakes and sponge cakes and things like that. It was amazing what women did to give variety to their foods. [With the rationing], all rubber things... You couldn't buy a pair of rubber overshoes, you know, that were made of rubber. You know your underpants have elastic around the waist, they did away with that. They were stitched around and buttoned on the side. *[Laughs]* I had a college friend, and she was very proper, you know, she was walking down the street one day, and the button fell off her pants. She was in the middle of the street. She said, 'I just stood there a minute and let them drop down and reached down and picked them up and went on.' *[Laughter]* But the babies, you see, babies [before rationing] would always have rubber bands. No rubber bands, they were not to be had. But...this was very hard on the mothers, there were no Pampers and things of that sort, you know. It was bad, the problem was very, very bad. The rubber was needed for jeeps and trucks that were part of the war effort, airplane tires and things, you see. So we knitted soakers, they were three corner pieces of wool yarn because wool holds the moisture and wool keeps you warm. Our bathing suits were all wool then because you get out of the water, and you wouldn't feel cold. But then they stopped all that, you know, when you got swimming pools. This was because wool has lint, and it would clog up the swimming pools. So now you don't have wool, very rarely would you find wool bathing suits. This sounds unbelievable but when you went to buy a tube of toothpaste it was in aluminum tubes you had to take back to get a new tube. That was because the aluminum then would be converted for the war effort. You gave in your old pots and pans that had holes in them. If they were aluminum, they would be reprocessed for that. Everything was converted to the war effort that was possible to do. We were very careful about coffee. You didn't waste coffee... but we always had some, but we drank a lot more tea probably, which wasn't so scarce.

Our clothes, the skirts were very short. Actually, the government regulated the width of the waistbands and belts and the pulls on the skirts, saving money on materials, the quality on material, you see. [*Pauses*] The quality of the materials was rather shabby too. We all wore hats; hats were very fashionable. A good hat would be made out of a fur product with a ...sheep hats were made just of wool and then they began to put other products in, you know. Another thing, our underwear was silk. We wore slips which were silk satin and they had to be ironed too, but they were nice. Our stockings were silk, nylon stockings didn't come in until about 1940. That was one of the big graduation gifts girls got when they graduated from high school, a pair of nylon stockings. They had seams in the back; you know you had to be very careful that your seams were straight, never twisted stockings. We rolled our stockings because with silk you could roll them. Of course girls got this habit of always pulling up their stockings, then when rayon came through you couldn't, you couldn't roll stockings because they would stay up. So that's where the two-way stretch came in and that had its problems too. I think back now and think probably the happiest moment of my day when I was teaching school was when I could get home and get the girdle off. Now girls don't wear things like that, you see.

Entertainment

Everything was kind of closed down, you know. You couldn't go any place because you didn't have a car [*Laughs*]. Quite different from today. We did not hear a lot. What was in the paper, what was on the radio. Lowell Thomas was on every night like, you know, like Dan Rather is now. They would tell us stories and then if you really wanted to see it, you went to the movies. We went to the movies a lot. It was cheap and you really got a good... You got the feature movie, and you got the previews, and you got the Pathé News.

The [Pathé] News would come on; it would show the ships that were being burned and the soldiers that were marching and the tanks that were down in the mud and all those things. That's the only way you got any pictures of anything, except *Life* magazine would come out with pictures. They would show a picture, that's why it was so popular. Oh, and at Christmas time, I think this must have been about Christmas of 1939, probably. The radio had a program where the children, the British children who had been sent to the United States for safekeeping could talk to their parents on the radio. It was just, it was just the most heart-wrenching experience. To hear these children seven and eight years old, you know, talking to their parents out there. But they had been sent here to be safe, you see, to be safe from the bombing. There were a lot of care packages too, at Christmas time. Even though you didn't know the boys, you know, you would collect them. The Red Cross did a lot of getting people involved in things. We also had airplane watch, you know, right on top of the school. Where every plane that went over, you reported it. They kept track of things. Of course, along the coast there were submarines and all kinds of things that people had to watch for.

Teaching

[The teacher shortage], well, that was very difficult. We had a lot of people in and out, in and out. Usually, they were people that were not successful from just the beginning. I think we had a lot of bad education. I remember at that time the state of New York enacted a law that all students had to take a health course. Who was going to teach it? Turned out that the home economics teachers were going to, because we all had a science background. We were very health conscious, we all had to do first aid. Home nursing courses, all the women did. Men and women took first aid courses. *[Laughs]* You had to learn how to do artificial respiration. They would get you down on the floor and push your chest and you'd be aching for about two weeks after that, but everybody did that. We rolled bandages, we knitted a lot, hats and scarves, and some did sweaters. We made bob cats, which were little toilet bags, and then filled it with things, you know. If you knew someone was in the service, you made a lot of cookies. Some goodies, you know, and tried to write letters. You keep writing to them to let them know what is going on here. The air raid drills, they were a big pain in the neck. In your high school today was one of the places that they had the air raid drills, you would hear things *[raises voice]* 'clang,' you know, and everybody would get up. Each homeroom had its assigned place, as I remember it. It wasn't your class you were in; it was your homeroom. You had an assigned place to be, it was all along the corridors, and it was inside the stage. All up against the wall, and you stood face to the wall and waited. Until…you were protected by the walls, you see, rather than being in the corridors. I don't remember if we had to get down on our hands and knees or not, but I don't think we did. But we did have to stand there until it was all over. It was like a fire drill in a way, but the rules were a little different. Some people had air raid shelters too, you know. They stockpiled canned food, sugar and milk, dry milk and so that when we had a bombing they would be protected. It was a very big fear, a very, very big fear later that Russia would bomb us. We lived with that!

[For first aid], well, we had to learn how to bandage. We had to learn about what we should use for certain problems. Bleeding was the main thing, and how to put a splint on if you had a broken limb and artificial respiration for drowning, you see. Also, how to protect against smoke inhalation and fires. *[Pauses]* I guess that was about it. Now, England, of course, had terrible air drills and lots of their families were lost. I know one young man who ended up in Bermuda and he lost his whole family. His mother and sisters and all of them, you see, the whole town would be wiped out. The bombings were so terrible, you see. The whole town would be wiped out, the bombings were so terrible in parts of England.

Then of course, you watch the newspaper because it would give a list of all the local people that had been injured or killed. All the towns had these big signs out, you know, of all the people in the town who were in it.

Roll of Honor, 1946, Hudson Falls High School yearbook photo, which stood before the town library.

Now, I don't know where Hudson Falls had theirs, but they must've had one that had a list of all the people who were joining the service. It also changed your social life for women particularly, because there wasn't anybody to go out with. Unless he was '4-F' and [Laughs] there was something 'with him,' you know. That was the first that women felt free to go to a restaurant or a movie unescorted. It was really rather an uncomfortable time, we weren't used to that, you know.

There were a lot of women that had always just stayed home and looked after the children. Now, they got out and got jobs and earned money. Of course it was Depression time too, so that extra money was wonderful to come by. One person would have a car, and everybody would pay him or her so much to ride to, say, Glens Falls. One of the places we had for women was McMullen's [three-story brick factory] that made men's shirts originally. Then it went into making women's dresses, very fine quality, very attractive dresses. The women learned very good sewing techniques by working in the shirt factories and the dress factory. Then a lot of women went to the [local] General Electric, located in Fort Edward, which wasn't too far, as they couldn't drive back and forth from [the main plant infrastructure] in Schenectady; GE took on a lot of people from this area.

We knew we were going to have sugar rationing, so my mother stored sugar! Now my mother canned a lot, she canned peaches and pears and she made jellies, and we needed sugar for those things, you know. So she...we had these great big tin cans, that I guess originally potato chips came in. They were probably ten gallons or so, they were like lunch pails, but were only metal. She would get sugar and put it up in the attic, so when necessity rose, we would have sugar. We never really did run out of sugar, but we were very careful. Soap was another thing, very hard to come by and you would be very careful with the soap. Of course, we didn't have laundromats and we didn't have automatic washing machines either. So you would have to wash with the old-fashioned washers with a spin dryer on it. If you had a modern one, it had a spin dryer and you would put it in this one to wash them, then you would take them out and put them in this, and it would spin them out. Then you could put them in a tub of water to rinse them, you know, then place them in the spinner to get the water out again so they would dry faster. No dryers either...even after the war.

My father [was a dairy farmer, and], yes, there were milk strikes. The price of milk was just terrible, just terrible, and farmers wanted more pay for their milk, so they went on strike. They called people who continued to sell their milk 'scabs.' Farmers normally would take their milk to the milk man, who was over there in Gansevoort, [near the railroad], right near where the post office would later be. A lot of men dumped their milk. But, of course, they were small dairy farms. Early on in my father's life they made butter. My grandmother made butter; I can remember it very well. She had butter customers in Glens Falls. So, my father just got out the old churn and made butter, we had plenty of butter! When the war was finally over, they raised the price.

Marriage During Wartime

There were a lot of quickie marriages. The boys would come home for a furlough and knew they were going back and felt if 'I don't get married... [pauses] and get this woman pregnant, I will have no offspring to carry on my name.' There were a lot of marriages of that sort. Then, of course, when the war was over, the marriage was no good. They just didn't get along. Then it started this terrible time with lots and lots of divorces and separations. There were a lot of girls who settled for anybody who came along because it was a time when every girl was supposed to get married, settle down and keep house. That was the main objective in many families. That all the daughters should get married, keep house, and have children. Then, when the war came and so many thousands of men were lost, there were not many available men of the quality that a girl would like—good education or talented—so they married whoever came along and that did not make for a happy marriage either when the war was over, because they didn't have anything in common. I will say, too, that there was a lot of drinking going on, terrible, not only during the war, but after the war. These men that came home, they were going to party and live it up. There was a lot of drinking going on. I think about that, and I think, how did anyone survive, because we didn't have laws about not drinking and driving. Cars were not as safe as they are now. Roads were not as well kept as they are now. But there were a lot of people who were killed too, but almost not as bad as they are now. Well of course they didn't have the speed that we have today. But there was a lot of drinking going on, which is very regrettable for both men and women. I was going with a fellow who was a metal artist, I didn't think much of it at the time. But he didn't go to war, and I know now that it was because he was a metal artist and the Americans didn't want him in the war effort, which he didn't talk about. Well, I didn't see anybody I thought I wanted to spend the rest of my life with. There wasn't too much to choose from. I had my chances but I'm glad I didn't take them. [*Laughter*] I don't regret it, no.

[After the war], we had the materials then to make clothes and make shoes and automobiles. My father kept saying… I didn't have a car, you see, of course, and he said, 'Well, as soon as the war is over, then they will make cars again.' They were not making any, so of course when the war was over, I was ready to buy a car. The price moved up considerably. My father said, 'If you only wait a year or two, the price will go down.' Of course, it didn't happen, so it was 1950 before I got my first car, and it was a brand-new Pontiac. I paid $1,700 cash for it, because I saved my money for it. That was my first car, some of the first cars that came out were very poorly made and very unsatisfactory. So probably waiting a little while didn't hurt, but there was a big boom. There was also a building boom, because there were no apartments, there were no houses being built. There were these young couples, that was the time when girls and young men were getting married, and then there was the baby boom. There was no place for them. My sister lived down there at the farmhouse for I think about two years while her husband was in the service. Then when he came home and they began looking for houses, it really was very, very hard. If you knew somebody who had died, then you would get a hold of the relatives to find out what was going to happen to the house. [Laughs] Then they started making and building a lot of houses too. Have you ever heard of Levittown? It's a very large town, city now, down on Long Island because that was near New York City, you see, and they needed houses. They built hundreds of houses in this area. They were all alike and they were all small houses. Beginners houses, you see, for these young couples that were getting married and having children. They had to have places and so the whole town was built. Schools were built, the whole thing. I wonder sometimes what happened to it.

The Boys in the War

[Several local families had their sons in the war], two brothers I knew, they both were Marines. One was in Guadalcanal and the other was in Iwo Jima. They both came home safely but they don't talk about it. This little project that you've got has probably started a lot of people talking. I have a magazine here, which I don't know where it is now, a little article in it about three men who have been in the war, and they were just beginning to talk about it now. So you're going to find out maybe a lot of things that people kept kind of in the background. My sister was in the Navy, my younger sister. During the WAVES, she was down in Virginia. Some of the folks that came in were a lot of burn patients. She doesn't ever talk about it. Of course, she wouldn't sail out of the country, either. [*Pauses*] She saw the men when they came home, and the condition they were in.

"'Four star mother,' probably Mary Marcantonio, the mother of four children, one adopted, who were all serving in World War II. Source: LOOK Magazine for 'Hometown USA' series, 1943-44. probably photographed by Harold Rhodenbaugh. The Folklife Center at Crandall Public Library, Glens Falls, NY.

I think at the time of World War II, [the draft] was very essential. There are a lot of people that wouldn't have gone into it if they hadn't been drafted. It was getting down to the point where they were going to draft men as old as 38, you know, which seems pretty old, but that's how hard up we were. All the young ones as soon as they got out of high school, they joined up. I remember one boy in particular we were very fond of, and he wasn't over there very long, and he was killed. He was probably nineteen, a lot of them very, very young. Mothers, little things they hung in the window, you know a little red, white, and blue sign and it had stars on it. When you had one son in you had one star, two sons, two stars, and so on. Then if you had lost a son, you had a gold star. You could go by the houses and see these gold stars and you would know where there were men in the service and who had lost sons.

I don't think [draftees] were eager, but I think the draft was very efficient. It was the Vietnam War where the men went to Canada and there was a draft then too, but somehow it wasn't as strict as it was in WWII. The feeling was totally different because of the Japanese. We were mad, and my sister, the younger sister, lives down in Georgia, is still mad. To some degree I am still indignant. I went to Japan on one of my trips. Beautiful country, friendly people, clean, very clean, but I didn't trust them. I'm not sure if I do today, I don't know. Marines were a tough bunch and you had to be ready to do all kinds of things to join the Marines. They were tough and a lot of them were sent to the Japanese war.

D-Day

I remember D Day with the most jubilation, and we got the day off. We got the rest of the week off, as I remember it. We were very happy. We knew it was coming. We didn't know about Normandy until it happened, you see. That was a very, very great secret. We did not know...We figured something big was going to happen, but we didn't know when exactly. It was a terrible thing for a lot of those fellows. In fact, to do all this embroidery I do, I took classes in Massachusetts, for several years I went after I retired. One time there was a man there and his wife had been interested in embroidery and he went with her, and he became interested. He had only one arm and he had been in the battle for three hours and lost his arm. He did very, very nice work with one hand. But he was maimed for life, you see, because the way it hurt his shoulder. No, he never did talk about that, he just said three hours and his arm was gone. It was a very violent thing, very violent.

These men keep going back, you know. Like the Marines they have meetings every year and then they go back to some of these places and see what has happened, you know. It was a terrible thing, so many of them so young, not much older than you are, you see. We had a family in Hudson Falls who lived over on the road to Hartford, a German family. I won't say the name because I might have the wrong name. But I remember the father's brother came over from Germany and they had been in the war over there. They had been deprived, of course. I seemed to remember another young man who had been taken prisoner. He was in the Air Force, that had come down and gotten into some German area, you know. He had been taken prisoner there, he got out of it eventually. [*Pauses*] We were all glad when it was finally over.

*

[When President Roosevelt died], we all knew he wasn't well, you could look at him and know he wasn't well. I was a Republican and I knew I made a mistake in feeling he had been in too long. He had been in for sixteen years, and previous to that he was Governor of New York State. So he was in the limelight for a long, long while. There was a slogan, 'You can't change horses in the middle of the [race],' which meant you can't change presidents while a war is on. That was one of the reasons he was put in year after year. It was to maintain his position to knowledgeably be able to help us with the war. He was probably the best equipped that we had. He wasn't afraid of Stalin, and he and Churchill were great friends, you know. But as he got older, he was less and less able to get out and around. They only showed us what they wanted us to see, they didn't want us to know he was in such poor health. That was probably smart.

Harry Truman was an entirely different kind of man. Roosevelt was a very highly educated man and spoke very beautiful English, you know. Harry Truman was just an ordinary man who had worked in a men's clothing store and sold suits and hats and things. I don't know how he ever got into politics the way he did. But he had a sign on his desk that said, 'The buck stops here,' and by golly, nobody could talk him into spending money that he didn't feel was right. He was actually a very good president.

'They Just Wouldn't Tell Anyone'

I think [the atomic bombing of Japan] probably was the only way to get things done. It was just going on and on and on. It ended things in a hurry. We spent a lot of time getting it ready. I knew of a young woman who worked at Oak Ridge. She didn't know what she was working on. So even the people who were making the parts for the atomic bomb didn't know about it, you see. The *Enola Gay* was the airplane that carried the crew that dropped the atomic bomb. It was named for the mother of one of the men on that plane. It was very, very, very secret. There was a lot of secret stuff that went on very, very quietly, part of it probably because we didn't have television because you know we've got people over in Iraq right now. Well, you probably watched it, sat right there in the truck with them while they're going down there towards Baghdad.

Now, [when servicemen returned from World War II], it wasn't that they were secretive about their experiences. No, they just wouldn't tell anyone. Well, if you were polite you wouldn't ask, you didn't try to dig it out of them. I think even their parents didn't know.

High school interviewer: So what do you think about the war today? The Iraq War?

I feel we had to do it for the safety of the world. I feel indignant that France and Germany won't help. After all, who were the troops that went marching into Paris when the war was over? Who was it that helped to get that Berlin Wall down? How much money did we put into all of this? Now this terrorism is a world-wide thing that has to be stopped. It's been an unexpected situation where we have been...we've lost many men and we've been badly hurt by it because their way of life is entirely different from ours and I don't think we've understood it. Also we're not always right, Americans are not always right. People don't always like us because we may appear to be cocky and superior and we're not always right.

I want to say this, too. When I was young, my grandfather would tell me stories, I didn't listen very well, now I wish I did, my grandma too, I didn't listen. How are we going to keep these things, don't you agree? They're very precious, really! Little things that I think about my grandparents, the little sayings that they've had.

Miss Washburn died on April 8, 2007, at the age of 89, three and a half years after this interview with my students.

CHAPTER SEVEN

The Schoolgirl

Elaine Sommo, born Elaine Curren, was the second of five children—all girls—who grew up in Vermont during the Great Depression. Her father was a steam shovel operator, and her mother worked as a waitress when times were tough. Like her older sister, she trained as a registered nurse. Elaine entered high school as the war began. Though too young to serve in World War II, she gave her teenage interviewer insight into her own teenage years during the war, her fears and dreams shared by a generation of young people across the United States. She sat for this interview in 2003 at the age of 75.

Elaine Curren Sommo

I was born in Fair Haven, Vermont, on March 26, 1928. I am now 75 years old.

During the Great Depression, goods and materials were short, however, we learned to get along without these things. A really vivid memory is that my father had a job at the Stasel Milling Company in Castleton, Vermont—they made roofing material. They would dig this material from the earth; my father ran a steam shovel. There was not enough work for civilians at the time, so he was transferred to Willimantic, Connecticut. My mother had five girls; I have an older sister ten years older than I, and the other four, starting with myself, have two-year differences in age, so we were all little girls. We took a train to Willimantic—we were there only three months—and then we returned to New Haven. The school we went to in Willimantic was called the Nantauk School, a wonderful school; we loved it. Two of my sisters were too young to go to school, but my sister, who is two years younger than I am, was in first grade and I was in third grade. To this day I still remember both the teachers' names, they were wonderful.

My father got a job with the WPA, the Works Progress Association. My father adored President Franklin Roosevelt, he thought that he helped a lot. I know that many people did not like Franklin Roosevelt, but I, to this day, like him. He also developed a program called the Civilian Conservation Corps. That was mostly for young men that needed jobs.

We received the daily paper. It was called *The Rutland Herald*, published in Rutland, Vermont. It was delivered to our door. I was frightened when I heard the news about Pearl Harbor. Our radio was on; it was on a lot, just like a lot of people have their televisions on. I was in the living room of our house in Fair Haven, and I could not believe it. I said to myself, 'We are going to be bombed!' I will tell you why I felt that way at thirteen. Germany had pummeled London, England, night after night after night—I do not know how London survived. This was all I could think of because we used to hear about it on the radio and the newsreels. I think we tried to act normally; I think everyone pretty much acted the same. We did the best we could with what we had, we got through it. At the time the war started, I remember being really afraid. As time went on, we had blackouts at night. We had dark green shades, and we had to pull them at night. One could not even light a cigarette on the street, or a flashlight, or anything, in case there were planes. Thank goodness. It was a terrible thing, there were so many hundreds of planes that bombed Pearl Harbor, the big carriers that came over. It was amazing, when I think of it, that we were not aware of it before it happened—that there was a possibility that it could happen. The Nazis especially impressed us a lot, they were the 'bad guys.' I think we heard more about them than the Japanese. [In school], I remember a quote, 'The only good thing about war is a geography lesson.'

The Victory Bike

We had a lot of rationing, of course. We had rationing stamps, which we got monthly. They were for basic things: eggs, sugar, and butter, actually I should probably say 'oleo.' It is what we had back then; oleo is substitute butter. It would come in a big brick, it looked like pure lard. We had a little yellow coloring thing that came with it. We had to let the oleo soften up, then mix in the coloring so we could use it. It was not the best tasting thing in the world, but we did get along, most people had it. We had a bicycle. In order to get a bicycle during [those times], someone, either your mother or your father, had to have it to go back and forth to work. That was the only way you could get one. We were a little underhanded in getting ours; my father said he would ride it back and forth to the Stasel Company, it was only three miles from Fair Haven. He rode it a couple of times and that was it; the bicycle was handed over to us girls. It was called a 'Victory Bike.' It had two wheels, handlebars, and that was about all; it was stripped of everything else. The tires were very, very thin due to the shortage of rubber. But four little girls had a very good time on that victory bicycle! We had it for quite a long time—sometimes there were arguments as to whose turn it was to ride it, but we managed. I guess that when you are faced with obstacles, like the Depression, it is like anything you are faced with that is not pleasant; you try to do the best you can with it.

I think how brave our parents were to have fed all those little mouths, maybe not knowing where all the food was coming from. They did have stations where you could pick up things like flour and sugar. We young girls were very proud and did not like to do that. We would go to this gentleman's house at night—we did not want anyone to see us, because we thought people would call us poor. We did not want to be known as poor. *[Laughs]* We did get through it, but, as I said, I do admire the parents; it was hard for them.

School

When I went into high school in 1942, we could not take typing because typewriters were short; you could not buy them. Soon after I graduated, things changed and typing started up. As the war went on, of course, young men went to war; help was short in every little town and city. It was apple-picking season, and Allen Orchards in Fair Haven had a huge orchard. They needed pickers. In the morning, they brought a big truck to school, we had lunch, and down we went to the orchard to pick apples. They paid us ten cents a bushel. I was never a very fast picker, but some of the kids were, and everyone tried to see if they could outdo the others. We did that for quite a few days; we thought we were helping the war effort; the young men were not around to do it.

In our park we had a big pile where you could put anything you had. Rubber was another thing as well. They needed all the rubber and metal they could get at that time for guns and equipment like tanks.

We lived in a home that did not have much yard, but my father worked for a gentleman who was in charge of a slate quarry in Fair Haven—a lovely man, he lived across the street from us, he had a huge garden. My father went over there and helped tend the garden for him; the gentleman was very generous. A lot of people had victory gardens; we just did not have the room. I know they did not have to be very big, but we did not have one. *[Laughs]* When we went to the pictures on Saturdays, they would always have a newsreel, quite involved. They would always show the planes bombing and this and that, all pertaining to the war. It was very informative.

There was V-mail, we did that; I think I wrote to a cousin. We wrote them and they were somehow reproduced on very thin, small paper, very fine print.

A teenage culture began to grow in America, as a result of the war. With labor shortages, teenagers were more able to get jobs early, earn money, and pursue a modicum of independence.

At thirteen, I started babysitting—my sister and I did a lot; I even babysat the child of my eighth-grade teacher. When I was older, I worked in a jewelry store in Fair Haven, and a bakery—I loved that, not just because it was a bakery, but because the people I worked for were lovely. I made fifteen dollars a week in the summertime, which was pretty good for only being fifteen years old. I did a lot of that until I was eighteen and went into training.

Now, I never really had a lot of extra money. I probably gave my parents some of the money. If we had extra money, then we had ten cents to go to the movie. The thing to do after school was to go down to the local drugstore and get a Coke float. *[Laughs]* We gathered there, and the gentleman who ran the pharmacy, the pharmacist, was wonderful to us kids. We behaved; we knew better than to act up. That was our thing to do. I loved sports, of course. I cheered for our team; I helped sell tickets to the basketball game. I was pretty active in high school; I joined in a couple of one-act plays, was president of my freshman class, treasurer of the senior class, belonged to the glee club—which a lot of people also did. In my senior year, I was an honors student and received the DAR award, which is quite a prestigious award. I never realized that until I was older—you were chosen by the faculty and your peers, quite an honor. I enjoyed school. One day I came here to the local high school and sat in on one of the classes. I thought, 'I wish I were back in school again!' [Laughs]

Culture and Music

[Frank Sinatra became popular during this period], but I did not like him. It took me years and years to like him. The thing I remember about him was that he had the microphone in front of him, and he was always shimmying up and down the pole. And he was skinny! I just did not like him, but in later years I learned to love him. We were all bobbysoxers. The girls wore skirts and peasant blouses, saddle shoes and ankle socks. That was the look back then, and it was fun. [Laughs] There was a sandlot near my home, and we played softball there. The boys and the girls played together and got along; there was not anything structured, anyone who was there played.

The Andrews sisters had a lot of songs, 'The White Cliffs of Dover,' 'When Johnny Comes Marching Home'; I am not sure if that is a World War II song, it might have been a Civil War.

[Laughs] There was a lot of Big Band music and sounds. Abbott and Costello were our favorites. When I look at them now, I wonder why we thought they were so funny. [Laughs] Judy Garland, Mickey Rooney, wonderful. MGM had a lot of beautiful musicals as well. We liked Tom Mix, cowboys, Gene Autrey. Those were the main ones when I was young. The girls especially liked Shirley Temple; Jane Withers was her friend. As we got older, we got to know some of the actors, Barbara Stanwyck, Ginger Rogers, and Fred Astaire. Some actress donated the bumpers off her car to a scrap metal drive. I think it was Barbara Stanwyck. [I remember the posters around during the war]; 'Uncle Sam Wants You!' 'Loose Lips Sink Ships' was another one. *[Laughs]* I remember when I was a sophomore in school, we had to write an essay on citizenship; I think it was, 'Duty, God and Country.' A boy and I won that essay contest. I wish I had it today, but you throw things away.

Elaine Curren during the war. Credit: Sommo Family.

The Neighborhood

[I did not know of any women who went to work in factories]; of course, there were no big factories in our area, not even Rutland. I do not know any young women in my area who did [factory work, but my mother was forced to become] a waitress. Back then, the men worked 12-hour days. We saw very little of the father, except on weekends. They all worked very hard. My older sister became like a mother to us, helped us get off to school, even though she had to get to school herself. We were very fortunate to have her.

In 1942, I was a freshman in school, and I developed a severe strep infection. I got to the point where I could not even move in bed; I had developed acetonemia, or, as the layperson would say, blood poisoning. My sister, Mary, had just graduated from the hospital in Rutland. Aqueous penicillin had not been on the market for very long—Sir Alexander Fleming discovered it way before 1939, when it was put on the market. My sister was available to give me injections every three hours; it saved my life. Mary was an RN—that influenced me more than anything. I have never regretted [becoming a nurse], although I have often thought about what it would have been like to be an English teacher.

[The neighborhood had an air raid warden]; they wore a patch on their sleeve and a hard hat. There was a group of men who did that. I knew there had been bombing—it was all we ever heard on the radio or at the movies—all this bombing, the V-2 rockets. I thought, 'They are going to come and that is all there is to it.' I was afraid; I was a child.

*

My [future] husband was nineteen when he was recruited. He went into the Army and became an MP, military policeman. He had not been there too long, when his contingent—most of them from Long Island, most of them nineteen years old—went right over to Europe. He did not talk much about it; a lot of servicemen do not. He would tell me, 'I was only just an MP, I did not do that much.' But they did have a lot of responsibility. They had to guard prisoners, direct traffic; I am sure there were other duties they had to perform. He was also in the African campaign. From the day he went into the service, it was three years until he came home again. He had a baby brother when he left, and when he came back, he was already three years old. Think how much a lot of men missed by going away.

We were sad when Roosevelt died. Very, very sad; anyone who liked him felt the same way. But when he met with Churchill and Stalin on that ship at Yalta, he was not well. He probably never should have been there; you could tell by his look. I never realized that until I was older, and if you see pictures of that you can tell he was not well. But he probably felt it was his duty and he had to go.

[When the atomic bomb was dropped], I had mixed emotions. I was thinking, 'What a terrible thing this is.' Another thought: 'If it is going to stop all this fighting, maybe it is okay.' But as I got older, I realized all the innocent people that it killed. Really mixed emotions.

'We Felt So Bad for Them'

[When the war ended], it was unbelievable; the country went wild, we were so thrilled. Everyone was happy and full of talk. For a small town we had quite a few fellows come back. I had two cousins that were over in Europe, they came back, and, of course, they had no jobs. They were not first cousins; they were my mother's cousins and we felt so bad for them. These two young men had mental and emotional problems until the day they died;

they could not get over it. It was very hard for them, one in particular. There were a lot of young men who hung around on the street corner; they had no place to go. They could go to the American Legion rooms, but as far as jobs, there was nothing for them. It was very difficult for a lot of them. It was also sad; a lot of men were killed. Some men from my town never came back, people you knew. In a small town, everybody knows everybody else. I felt very thankful, glad and sad.

There were problems, but we coped the best we could. We did not get all bent out of shape; we went along with what had to be done. I'm not sure I am in total agreement with the phrase, 'The Greatest Generation'; perhaps not the greatest, but a great generation. I think there were other generations that had to go through terrible times of war and famine. I would not want to brag and say we are the greatest, but I think we were great. Later on after the war, things picked up, jobs came along. People went about doing what they had to do. Goods were more available, but it took a little time. Of course, we were happier. We were glad to see the war over and hoped it would never happen again. I think General Douglas MacArthur did a grand job over there; it certainly was not easy for him. I think he was a wonderful commander. Patton and Eisenhower, General Mark Clark, they are the other ones I remember the most. I think that they were very intelligent men, knew their job, and carried it out to the best of their ability. Maybe a lot of people would not agree with me, but that is my thought.

High school interviewer: Do you think, in the midst of all the destruction the war brought, the world became a better place?

Hopefully it did. I would hate to say, 'No, it did not.' It is too bad that we have to have war in order to make things better, but it has been that way since time began. I have mixed feelings about [the idea of parents having to] send their children off to war. I probably did not even think of it then; I was so young. If there is a conflict, it would be terrible for a parent to send a child off to war. But in another vein, somebody has to do it. It is not very pleasant, that is for sure.

I think the war made everyone stop and think, to maybe make you a better person, in trying to make sure it does not happen again. [As for women's rights], if women can do that economically, [it follows that social change [would come], toward equality to men. I never believed we had to be subservient to a man. But I think the women's rights groups carried it a bit too far, they have to have this and that, and they have to join men's groups. What harm is there in a man having his own group? Why do we always have to be intermingled? We can still get along.

We lived through the war and got along, and we are here to talk about it. But like any parent with children, you want the best for them, and the safest for them, and the kindest for them. It would be kind of hard to watch your children's generation go through it again. Let us hope we, especially you, growing up, do not have to go through anything like that.

We survived; you either survive, or you sink. You can get up and do something about it, or you can sit in a chair and wither away.

CHAPTER EIGHT

The Pearl Harbor Kid

Mr. Spencer Kulani was born in Brooklyn, New York, in 1935. As a child after the attack on Pearl Harbor, his family moved to Oahu, Hawaii, where he spent most of his childhood. Much later, he enlisted in the Marine Corps and was stationed at Camp Pendleton, but his formative memories were as a child living near Pearl Harbor at his family's restaurant. He sat for this interview in January 2006 with one of my students at the age of 70.

Spencer Kulani

On December 7, 1941, I was in Brooklyn, New York, on 53rd Street and 3rd Avenue. We had just come out of the movies, and we were going to a candy store. We were on our way to Chinatown, and we went to the candy store to buy some gum because the young lady that was with us had motion sickness, and she had to chew gum while she was on the subway. And when we went into the store, we had heard on the radio that Pearl Harbor had been attacked; that was in the afternoon when we got the news.

Family in Pearl Harbor

I was really too young to really realize. All I knew was that my brother was over there. Most of my emotions were taken off of [being near] my father; whatever emotions my father had, I had them too. As far as my own emotions are concerned, if he would have smiled and laughed, I probably would have smiled and laughed. I was really too young to really realize what was going on.

My parents were hurt and worried about my brother because he was in Pearl Harbor at the time; [we had family there.] Al was probably twelve years old at the time, and they were more worried about him and the rest of the family. But as far as other people around me and how they reacted, I really do not remember. The big thing was we really had food [rationing] stamps and such, buying meat, but it never really affected us as kids, but it did affect the family. We had victory gardens going and drives for tin cans, rubber drives and all kinds of waste material that they would put in a pile where scraps would actually be. They had scrap drives and then they would have victory gardens for people to have enough land to plant their food and stuff. That is about all I saw as far as support; I mean you always have the flags out, of course, and such.

Around December 1942, we got on the bus from New York to go to Hawaii, we left for San Francisco by bus. My dad was a musician, and we got a flat tire in some state, I do not remember which state. We spent about six hours on the side of the road waiting for someone to come fix the flat tire on the bus. My dad played music and the guys played cards and everyone just had a good old time traveling by bus. We got to San Francisco and stayed in a hotel most of the time while we waited for transportation to go to Hawaii; you had to wait your turn until you got a ship that left San Francisco that left for Hawaii.

Going Across the Pacific

There were a lot of civilians on the ship that we were on, an awful lot. And a lot of them, mostly, I imagined were defense workers going to work in the shipyards, welders and the like, people that did not actually qualify for the actual service or were too old for the service.

Going across we all ate at the big chow table; we were just like servicemen. The ship was made and built for servicemen, and we ate just like them. The seas got rough, and they had blackouts, the lights went out on the ship, they shut all the doors. You could not open any of the doors on the ship at night, everybody had to stay inside, except of course for the crew, and they had big canvases. They would open the door and first they would step in the hallway, close the canvas, then open the door so no light could get outside. They were worried about submarines attacking the boats and stuff like that. But it was a good cruise, I had a lot of fun. There was no big fanfare when we got to Hawaii; there was no Hawaiian aloha band or anything like that. We just docked and everyone just got off the ship and that was it. There was no fanfare. It was the first time I had ever been there.

Pearl City

The land we lived on in Hawaii was called Pearl City Peninsula. Before the war my grandmother was leasing the land off a big and rich family, and when the military came, they said, 'You cannot have this land, it is going to be turned over to the military.' They just took it away from her. Financially they gave her the money for what she leased it for, but it was not hers no more. We had what they called Queen's Pond right there in Pearl Harbor. When we were kids we used to play in it; the Navy filled it all in and made docks and piers for the ships to pull up and load and unload. They made a big storage area out of Pearl City down in the peninsula, which is for cargo ships. That is how it changed.

Pearl City's peninsula is in Pearl Harbor. We stayed there from 1943 until we left in 1946, and that was after the war. And it was one of those things that happened and as the war progressed things got easier. We did not have food stamps, not there, not in Hawaii. But they had an old car, and gas was hard to get; they had some aviation gas off the airport over there and they stuck it in the old car and burned up the valves because the aviation gas was too much of a high octane. It burned up all the valves in the car, had to get a valve job on it. But they needed gas to move the car. That is one of those things you know you do.

[Coming from Brooklyn], well, Hawaii was just a lot of fun. I mean, you were living in New York, you needed a lot of clothes, but in Hawaii you went barefoot, things like that. You hardly ever wore a shirt, especially when you are kids. Nobody wore shoes over there, you had to get used to that. It took about six months before you could walk the way everybody else could walk, until it did not hurt your feet as much, but there were kids over there that could put cigarettes out on the bottom of their feet, that is how tough it got out there. All in all, as a kid, it was just one big party. You go to school just like any school. You had air raid drills where they would run everybody, once a week, under the bomb shelter, which is a hole dug in the ground about six feet down. Then they would just put a big mound over it with wood and you would crawl down inside. They would have big benches, and everybody would just sit down and look at each other, sit there for about five or ten minutes, then they would blow the alarm, and everybody would come out. That is the way they [practiced for] war in school. Of course, we had victory gardens and stuff like that. Most of it was playing, they had a big dump, and they would dump everything they had, new ball bearings, parts of airplanes; of course, we kids would go through it to see if we could find anything. Things like that, you would just ride your bike. There was no restriction on us, we just went wherever we wanted to go. Of course, the only place you could not go was the Navy base, and you cannot do that today.

Martial Law

When Pearl Harbor was attacked it then became a martial law, which means the military has more say than anyone else on the island. It was their law, there were guys that got shot because they did not stop, and the military shot them. But they were scared of spies because there was an awful lot of Japanese at the time. I do not think, in all the people in Hawaii that were Japanese, I do not think they found one Japanese that was ever a spy or ever proved that there was a Japanese in Hawaii that was a spy.

Most of the Japanese in Hawaii were hurt, just like the rest of the people. That was their home and to have their own country bomb their own home hurt them. The people in Hawaii, the Hawaiian people, the Japanese, the Filipinos, the Orientals, and the whites, they all got along pretty good, the people that knew Hawaii. The servicemen that came there had a lot of what you would call 'hate' because with some of the Japanese Americans, all they would see is Japanese, but they did not care. It is just like today a lot of people see Arabs, and they get all excited, and blame the Arabs for everything; they get all shook up about Muslims, but every Muslim is not the same, they all do not believe in killing everybody. The same thing happened in Hawaii, and as most people know a lot of Japanese in this country, they were put in a concentration camp; now, they did not say it was a concentration camp, but more or less that's what it was. But in Hawaii they did not do that to them; half the people over there were probably [of Japanese descent], they could not stick half the island in a concentration camp. But they proclaimed martial law, and the military took care of their own. Of course, the Hawaiian police took care of their own too. We had curfews and stuff like that, but for most of the people it was good, as far as us kids go it was really good, but you know older people are different.

'Their Hair Had Turned White'

I had about four cousins who were all in the service; most of them were in the Navy. They were all in the European theater. Most of the rest of the family worked in Pearl Harbor, there was a restaurant and a bar, but that is all. That is all we ever did, work. You know there are different things that happened to them over there; when we got there, most of them had been through the attack at Pearl Harbor. There was the old fellow, grandfather, step-grandfather actually, he just passed away two years ago, he was 103 years old. He was born in 1901 and he had talked about different things that happened to him on the day of the attack on Pearl Harbor. He was saying that when Pearl Harbor was attacked, all the civilian workers ran for the gate, they wanted to get out of there, but the military stopped them from leaving Pearl Harbor because they needed people to repair and fix the area. He said when they all attacked, they were working on the different ships in the area, and he had got behind a telephone pole and he had got strafed by a Japanese airplane, they were just strafing the whole area. And he said that he had thought that he had been shot, but what had happened was the bullets hit the gravel around his legs, and he thought they had hit his legs with the bullets, but it was just the gravel that hit him in the leg, and he got all excited about that. Then they kept him there all night and he said that in the middle of the night, he would go over there to all the secretaries. He went over to the side of the building and picked up a bunch of gravel and he threw it on the roof. It sounded like bullets hitting the roof, and they all got underneath the desks and he stuck his head in and started laughing at them. Of course, they did not appreciate that one.

About twenty years later he had worked for the bank and one of the women that made out the bills was one of the women that was inside that building when he threw the gravel up. She had called him up and said, 'Are you that stinker that threw that gravel on the roof, I was in Pearl Harbor.' And of course, they got together, and they had a good time, they had dinner and all that, but it was just remembrance.

Those were different things that people remember about Pearl Harbor. He said that a lot of the boys got stuck in the ships. Phil was in supplies and what they would do was, they would supply the different ships with the different everything, food and stuff. And a lot of the young sailors would come by and get the supplies from the ship, and he says a lot of them are storekeepers on the ship. And a lot of those kids got stuck in the bottom of the ship. They got them out, but a lot of their hair had turned white, that's how scared they were. Which was a hell of an experience, stuck in a hole underneath water, figuring you would never get out of it. A lot of kids came out with white hair, and they were only 19 and 20 years old. Those were the different things that happened there.

'This Was Their Last Chance'

My dad worked in the family restaurant as a bouncer when he got over there, because my grandmother had a restaurant and he worked for the shipyard for a little while as well. The servicemen, most of it was just party time, really. Servicemen came in and all they wanted to do is eat, sleep, and drink, they figured this was their last chance. They would have a big party and they figured if they left Hawaii, they would be dead, so all they wanted to do was party. A lot of them did not even come back. The family had quite a few friends in the restaurant that did not make it back. Owning a restaurant like that, you see a lot of servicemen, but me myself, we were all kids then, it was no big deal for us. We would just go down to the beach, and we would watch them load ammo, doing whatever they were doing.

I saw two planes crash up in the air when I was a kid. We were out there swimming in a swimming pool and two guys up there in the air, we could see they were chasing each other, and all of a sudden, they turned around, and both of them came together and boom, they just collided in the air. I saw one of the men's parachute come out and down he went. I do not know what ever happened to the other guy; of course, I did not read the paper back then.

'Just One of Those Things'

As far as war stories go, these guys would come back; in a bar one time, a jarhead he was, and Indian, he came back and he had a Japanese ear inside of a bottle of alcohol, it was his souvenir. People talk about how rotten the different countries are and how nasty they did things. If you talk to some of these guys that had really been over there, they did some bad stuff over there. They were actually giving bounty for the ears. From what I understand they wanted to go out and get the snipers, they were giving money for the ears. So these guys would go out and hunt these Japanese down and kill them and cut their ears off so they could get some money. And that is how they got the Japanese snipers, because nobody wanted to go out there. This is a story, I have no written proof of all this, but I did see that ear come in in a jar, and I understand what was going on, that is how they got the Japanese snipers out of there. They had to stop it because these guys were going and cutting ears off of dead guys and tried to come back and tried to claim the money for them. In reality, we may not have started it, but we did some awful things, things that a lot of the guys are not proud of, but that is all a part of war, it is just one of those things.

The End of the War

After the war ended, they had a USO club. Well, actually before the war ended, they had gotten together with Love's Bakery and made what they called already-made sandwiches. That was one of the first civilian outfits on base that delivered lunches. I do not know what you call them; you see them in convenience stores, prepackaged sandwiches. They were the first ones to make them, and my dad used to deliver them to all the different Navy facilities; he would go out there, making deliveries of sandwiches. At the end of the war, my father was offered a machine gun, a rifle, and the guys were just giving them away because the guys were so happy that the war was over. They did not have to be accounted for, so they were going to give them to all of them. He did not want any of it, they were all automatic weapons, and he knew it was against the law to have them, so he did not touch any of it. But those were the things that happened, but when the actual war ended, I was in Pearl Harbor and they were firing live ammo in the air, shooting all over the place, shooting live ammunition all over the sky when the war ended.

Back In New York

After the war was over, we ended up back in New York. And then, of course, we stayed there a little while and things did not go well so we ended up back in Hawaii again. We stayed there until the Korean War started. So, I probably came back here to New York from about 1946 until about 1948, then we went back to Hawaii in 1951. That is about the time I spent in Hawaii. I went back there in 1985 and we tried to get down in there and they would not let us in there anymore. I just wanted to see what it looked like, but you had to be in the military to get down there and of course I was not so they would not let me down there. A lot of USOs turned into different night clubs. The military still had a good hold in Pearl Harbor. Now the sugar cane companies are all folding up, I think they are getting outsold from Mexico, I think that is what's happening there. A lot of the farms and all that, now they are going to coffee. Their land is very fertile; they can get three crops of corn in Hawaii in one year. Now they cannot get sugar, they cannot get any money for their sugar, and the mangos, and the pineapples, and the papayas. They are all coming out of South America and Mexico. Actually Hawaii, before World War II, was the third largest beef producer in the world for export. Parker Ranch had a million-acre ranch on the island of Hawaii. And they were the third largest export producer of beef in the world. Of course, Argentina and the US were fighting for first place. Hawaii was really considered a territory during World War II, it was not part of the United States as a territory, like Puerto Rico is today. In fact, we had American money in Hawaii that was all stamped 'Hawaii' on it and that is what they used for currency, and it was illegal to bring it to this country. It was the same money that you have today, of course there was that silver certificate, but it was the same money you have today only it had 'Hawaii' stamped across the front of it. If you have got any of them now, they are worth a little bit of money.

*

What else can you say? I think World War II was a necessity and there is no getting away from that. You have to talk to some of the guys over there, who have been there and done it. Especially some of these guys that were ground troops, they are the ones that know what it is really all about. Of course, I was a kid and I had fun; they did not, but I did. We used to go along the beaches, and you would find washed-up C-rations on the beach. We found life rafts made out of balsa wood; we would cut up the balsa wood and make little boats out of them. In fact, there was a lieutenant in the Navy who would carve boats for us. He made some beautiful models for us, and it was all out of these balsa wood rafts. You would go along the shore and cans of C-rations, you would open it up and there would be candy and of course we would eat them. They all floated in from a sunken ship, who knows where it came from? You would find them on the beaches all the time, in Pearl Harbor, all along, all along the beaches in Hawaii. That was some of the different things I remember; [in the big picture], when you are a kid you do not realize what is going on.

Spencer Kulani passed away in November 2022 at the age of 87.

PART THREE

SERVICE

"There was one psycho case who saw ducks, he was in New Guinea, wherever he went he saw ducks. Well, the psychiatrist tried to rid him of the ducks. Finally, they sent him back but he still saw his ducks. They decided, he's no good, we'll send him back to the States as a Section 8. Well, it's four hours from New Guinea to Guadalcanal, another twenty hours to Hickam Field, another fourteen hours to San Francisco. All of this time he saw his ducks. Finally, about an hour out from San Francisco he calls the flight nurse over and said, 'Lieutenant, you can have the ducks now, I don't need them anymore.' [Laughs]"

—Flight Nurse, Pacific

CHAPTER NINE

US Army Nurse, Europe

Kathryn Goodman Frentzos was interviewed several times by my students for this project. Raised in a very rural Adirondack Mountain setting, she rose to the rank of major during the war.

Kathryn Goodman Frentzos

I was born on September 20, 1912, in Athol, Warren County, New York. I have two sisters and four brothers. Three of my brothers went into the service, one in the Pacific and two in the European theater. I was the second oldest. Both of my sisters were also nurses.

The Depression Era

My first few years I grew up in Johnsburg, New York; it's a small, little village, really a hamlet, in the Adirondack Mountains. It was just like a wide place in the road, a few houses and a grocery store, a post office, and they also had a cobbler, that sort of thing.

I had a rather routine childhood. We didn't have electricity in our house, until like sometime in the 1930s when Roosevelt became president and the Rural Electrification Act was passed, then we had electricity, and we got a bathroom in our house and things like that. Growing up during the Depression didn't bother us at all. Some people were better off. But I lived on a farm when I was growing up and we always had food because we had a garden. And we had chickens, and we had a cow, so we always had milk and we really didn't suffer. We just thought everybody was poor, like us, but of course that wasn't true, but we did very well during the Depression.

I really had only seven years of grammar school, because at the end of the seventh year, the teacher asked me if I wanted to take the eighth-grade Regents [examination]. So, I took the eighth-grade Regents, and I passed them, and I went into high school right out of seventh grade! I had four years of high school and four and a half years of college, so I had, you know, a pretty good education.

'Once You Do This, You're Theirs'

I graduated from North Creek High in 1929. From September 1931 to January of 1932, I attended Albany State Teacher's College intending to become a teacher. The courses I liked best in college were anatomy and physiology, and I decided I'd rather be a nurse; accordingly I applied to and was accepted as a student at St. John's Long Island City Hospital School of Nursing. I graduated in September 1935, took and passed my state board examination and became a registered nurse. My nursing career took me from general duty nursing at Polyclinic Hospital in New York City in 1935 to the Albany visiting nurse service from 1937 to 1940. While attending teacher's college at Columbia University, fall session 1940, on a New York State scholarship, I saw a recruiting poster urging nurses to join the Army Nurse Corps. I was interested, so I immediately joined the Red Cross Nursing Service, which was a prerequisite to joining the ANC. Soon I was requested to make an appointment at 90 Church Street in New York City to take a physical exam. I was a little less than five feet tall, but the examining physician, who wasn't that tall himself, told me to stand as tall as I could. I just barely made the height to pass.

When I joined up, my father was a little bit concerned because he said, 'Kathryn, once you do this, you're theirs, you know, you belong to them. You don't have any say in what's going to happen to you,' which was true. You went where they sent you. They owned you.

Pearl Harbor

I took my oath of office on February 21, 1941, and then took a standard train to Tennessee. When we got to Camp Peay, the name had been changed to Camp Forrest. I stayed there for twenty-two months, during which I was promoted to first lieutenant and eventually to captain.

On December 7, 1941, I was still in this country, and I remember that day very well, it was a Sunday, and I was going off duty at three-thirty in the afternoon and the nurses coming on duty were crying and I said, 'What's the matter, what happened?'

They told me that Pearl Harbor had been attacked by the Japanese. Well at that time I had no idea what Pearl Harbor was, I didn't know that it was an Army base in the Pacific, actually. [Later], the nurses in the [Philippines] were not so well taken care of. They were in [the service of] of General MacArthur, and MacArthur [later] got on a submarine and went to Australia and left his soldiers and his nurses there at the mercy of the Japanese.

Several months after my promotion to captain, I received orders in early December to proceed to Camp Kilmer, New Jersey, to join the 500 bed 40th Station Hospital in the unit as chief nurse.

Overseas

Camp Kilmer was the pits. It was the least accommodating, the most uncomfortable billet I have ever experienced in my five years in the service. I joined my unit on December 6, and on December 12, we boarded a troop ship for an unknown destination. Throughout the voyage we were required to wear helmets and life preservers and to carry canteens full of water at all times. We had many lifeboat drills also; we sailed under strict blackout conditions. We were constantly in danger because we were on the ocean between America and North Africa, which was constantly being patrolled by German submarines, and we never knew when we might meet German ships and then be conquered by them. The ship ride over was an experience in itself. Because we sailed from New Jersey, about three days' out we got a storm at sea, it was really a very bad storm. And on the tables that we ate at, they put rims around the edges to keep the dishes and the food on the table and everybody got sick, but I think I was the only one of the nursing and doctor's staff that didn't get sick, and our chief surgeon always said after that I kept him alive; I saved his life. Well, I didn't do anything to save his life except to tell him, 'Don't eat anything except crackers!' And he always swore that I saved his life.

We had to have helmets on all the time while we were on the ship, and we had to have a canteen always filled with water in case you had to get off the ship and get onto the lifeboats, where there would be no drinking water. Of course we didn't have any lights on at night because we were traveling in a convoy with other ships, and there were German ships all over the waters, but we never had any problems, we got there safely.

North Africa and Corsica

When we reached Oran, in Algeria, on December 25 of 1942, we couldn't depart until the next day because French Admiral Jean Darlan had been assassinated in Algiers on Christmas Eve and it wasn't clear what kind of reception we would get.[10] We did have a traditional Christmas dinner on board the ship on Christmas Day.

We were in Algeria, then French North Africa, for thirteen months where we lived in old French foreign barracks. Finally, we went by plane to the island of Corsica where we stayed in several locations.

As a chief nurse, I was in charge of 55 women. We went from 250 patients to 500. So, as the war went on, we got more and more patients, our hospital got bigger. And sometimes our hospital was in tents. And other times it was in buildings. For example, in Corsica, we were in tents all the time. And that was interesting. One time we had a big wind blow through it, and it blew down all of our tents. Nobody got hurt, but we had to put the tents up again and put everything back in order. There were three types of hospitals. There were field hospitals, which were sort of like *M.A.S.H.* units; you know, you must've watched *M.A.S.H.* on television? Well, there was that, and then there were station hospitals, and then beyond us were the general hospitals, they were closer to home, not physically closer, but the soldiers were closer to [get-

---

[10] *French Admiral Jean Darlan*- Pro-German Vichy French naval commander-in-chief in North Africa.

ting] home. While we weren't exactly like *M.A.S.H.*, which was a Mobile Army Surgical Hospital unit in the war area, we did have the mail call [you see in the television series], and mail call was the most important time of the day because you might be getting letters from home. I got letters from my brother John, who was the oldest of my three brothers who were in the service, in the Pacific theater, in the Navy. We wrote letters back and forth but that was all. We had no personal contact. We were too far apart.

World War II was an unusual experience, because the ordinary person doesn't get to go overseas and work in tents and such. At one time our hospital was set up in a small hotel and an apartment house and in a school, a children's school. You did your work every day; we had things to do and you did them and I had to see that the nurses did what they were supposed to do because as a chief nurse, that was my job. For our overseas duty the nurses were all adequately clothed in government-issued duty uniforms and outerwear. We always had sheltered living quarters whether in tents or buildings, and toilet facilities with latrines if we lived in tents or regular bathrooms if we lived in buildings. Food was adequate and well prepared and good; we used our mess kits only occasionally when we were breaking camp in our location and preparing to move. The hospital, wherever the setting was, provided all the necessary equipment. The welfare of all the personnel was a priority, from the commanding officer down through the ranks. We didn't get homesick because we were so busy all the time. You know, when you're nursing you have wards full of injured people; you don't really have much time to do anything except work.

When the soldiers came to us, they had already had first aid and they were bandaged, you know, whatever immediate care they needed they had and they came to us and it was just like any other hospital that you would work in. You give them whatever care they need and you try to get them healed so they can go back to duty, but sometimes they went on to another hospital, which was called a general hospital, and if they couldn't get the soldier to go back to duty, they sent them home. We had an adequate staff for the daytime shift, the afternoon shift, and the nighttime shift. The nurses wanted to work around the clock, but in the effort to keep them from getting sick or too tired out, we kept them to their regular schedule.

When we had days off, we usually had two days off, I think, so we went on trips to other places in the area and we saw whatever scenery there was to see wherever we were. We had recreation, we had dances, and of course there were so many more men than there were women, that we were never without a date if we wanted to go.

One memory that sticks out [in Corsica] is that in June of 1944 [just before D-Day], when they had the battle in southern France, we got a shipload of soldiers who had been wounded in that. They came to us, and they were mostly burn cases because they had jumped into the ocean and the ocean was literally on fire, so they got burned. When they came to us they were wrapped in medic's [bandages] and probably only a little bit of their faces was showing and they looked like the Michelin Man, you've seen pictures of the Michelin Man?[11] That's what they looked like, and they were youngsters, German soldiers, they were fifteen, sixteen years old or so, they were like our little brothers, you know? And their shoes were so thin, there were holes in them, you know, and Germany was running out of everything then, so that battle was really the end of the war for them. At our triage point they were sorted, and the ones that were the worst off were taken care of

---

[11] *Michelin Man-* mascot of the Michelin tire company, a bloated human-like figure consisting of stacked white tires, introduced in France in 1894.

first, and that was when my nurses wanted to work all night, no matter what their normal tour of duty was, they just wanted to work all night because there was so much to do, but I had to let them work just their shift and let another shift come on, so they wouldn't get exhausted.

After the Battle of the Bulge, which began on December 16 of 1944, we were again on the move, this time to Italy outside of Rome. We lived and set up our hospital in what had been Musso-lini's glass factory, where all personnel of the hospital were housed in buildings.

Mt. Vesuvius

I have one very fond memory; people are always surprised when I tell them this. We had a colonel who was the head of our unit and there were other men who were assistants of his, and one day a general came to visit our colonel and he had lunch with us. He said to the colonel, 'I would like to take you on a trip down over Mt. Vesuvius this afternoon,' and of course being the chief nurse, I was asked to go, too. So, he had a B-17 with a plexiglass nose, and when we go into the plane, it was the control room, we got into the plexiglass nose and I had to lie on my stomach so I could see everything, and so he took us down over Mt. Vesuvius, which of course is a volcano, you know churning and burning and all, whatever burns in there. Well that was really interesting, and being in the nose of a B-17 was like being on a magic carpet and that was really the highlight of all the things I did. After that we flew back up over the north of Rome, over the Pope's summer palace, Castle Gandolfo.

The End of the War

While we were in other countries, if you were an officer, enlisted men had to salute you and it was very funny when they would see me with the captain's bar on my hat and so forth, and they'd say, 'Ma'am/Sir?' They were surprised and they would do a double take and then they would salute, because they weren't used to saluting women.

We were all very sad when Franklin Roosevelt died. A lot of us had never had any other president other than Franklin D. Roosevelt and we were very sad that he had died. It was like losing a close relative. Germany surrendered unconditionally in May of 1945, so the war in the European theater was over. In July 1945, after nine months of living in Rome, we moved to Naples. We did not set up a hospital in Naples; most of the time was spent watching training films and wondering what was next for us. The plan was that those with the longest length of service would eventually go home, and others would be sent to the Pacific theater. However, that never happened, because on August 14, the Pacific war was over and eventually everyone was sent home.

'What Are You Going to Do For Me?'

[When the war finally ended], I was very, very happy. I didn't like the idea of so many people being killed [by the atomic bombs], but the other thing about that was we were really told that it shortened the war, so it saved a lot of lives also. But things had changed when we got back home. You know before I went in the service, if I went somewhere to get a job my question was, 'What can I do for you, what do you expect from me?' you know. After the war when I came back and I worked again in the hospital, when they had people coming looking for jobs, their questions were, 'What are you going to do for me?' instead of 'What can I do for you?' to get a job, you know, 'What do I get out of this?' It was a very different attitude.

'They Are Mostly Gone'

In November of 1946, I was promoted to the rank of major. My post-war nursing experience was all in teaching and administration. The most rewarding thing [to come out of my experience, for me], was that I had a profession in which I could help people, sick people and wounded people. It's pretty hard to just tell somebody, in a couple of hours, about the war. One thing is that we were always treated very well; the nurses were treated extremely well, which wasn't true in the Pacific theater. It's pretty hard to describe the war, but I wouldn't have missed serving in it. I was very happy to be able to serve in the war. I kept in contact with some of the nurses [after the war]; I did that for a long time. But they're mostly gone; I think the ones I kept in contact with are all gone. You know, World War II nurses and soldiers are dying off at a very fast rate. You won't find very many 99-year-olds like me. I'll probably live a couple more years anyway. [Laughs]

Nobody ever asked me anything about my service except when I first came home, I went to church one Sunday with my father, and some little girl came up to me and said, 'Did you ever ride in a jeep?' [Laughs] That's the only question anybody ever asked me. But you know, when I was in the service, times were not so good here either, because everyone was on rationing, shoes were rationed, certain foods were rationed, sugar was rationed, but we had everything we needed overseas. People in America were rationed, and they had blackouts—as we did, of course. Another thing that I found out after I came home—I didn't know it when I was in the service—there was a big tent on our front lawn, and I said, 'What in the world is that?' They said it was for plane spotting, and there were people in the community who would come to our house to spot planes going over, and the tent where they stayed was still on our front lawn! And I didn't know anything about it while I was overseas, nobody thought to tell me or write me or anything about it. So, people here didn't have it too easy either, they suffered probably more than we suffered, because we really didn't suffer, we were extremely well taken care of. And I've always been so happy that I had it so good, believe me.

Kathryn Goodman Frentzos passed away on June 2, 2015, at the age of 102.

CHAPTER TEN

US Army Nurse, Pacific

Katherine Denegar joined the Army Nurse Corps after Pearl Harbor, serving in the Pacific theater in the Philippines. Like most of our women veterans, she was motivated to serve her country, but even after the war she had to deal with pushback from a veterans organization that denied her a membership, solely because she was female. She set the record straight, refusing to join with auxiliary status. She sat for this interview in 2003, just before her 87th birthday.

Katherine G. Denegar

I was born in Youngstown, Ohio, in 1916. [By the time of the war], I was a registered nurse, and I also had a bachelor's degree in psychology. [I remember that when I heard about Pearl Harbor], I was working nights and I just couldn't believe it, it's like yesterday; you don't forget these things. We were all, of course, terribly excited when we got into the war and realized the damage that was done to our Navy.

I enlisted in Youngstown, Ohio. I knew the Army nurses went overseas and at that time I didn't think the Navy nurses did and I just liked the Army. I had further training when we went to Fort Knox, Kentucky, and then of course I had the usual training that they give you; in other words, crawling on the ground, the whole thing, even marching. I did a terrible job because I'm left-handed and left-footed and everything else, but the second lieutenant passed me. I guess they were desperate.

'I Would Kill You'

We had basic training at the hospital, them telling us, 'You know how to do your work, but now you do it the Army way,' and we understood it from that. The first thing after I left Fort Knox, Kentucky, I went to Newton D. Baker Hospital in Maryland, and that I think is mostly psychology. And unfortunately, the major there wanted to keep me as a psychiatric nurse, and I had never done it and she said, 'Well, you have a bachelor's in psychology; you could do quite well.' But I was put in the most mentally disturbed ward. Which was quite an unhappy situation. You realize what war is like when you see these men coming back like that, as a result of the European theater mostly. I had never had psychology, all I had was the study of the different diseases in psychology, and to go into this most mentally disturbed ward, I remember feeding a young, very strong-looking man and he said, 'You're pretty, but if I could get you, I would kill you.' I mean, we had that sort of problem, and we had these catatonic patients that would stand for hours at a time and then rush and try to destroy their beds, that sort of thing.

I read a lot of their histories, which I found very interesting. This one particular man that was catatonic had been made to bury the dead in Europe and he just couldn't handle it. I also realized by reading all their histories, that some of them should have never been in the Army, but with the excitement of World War II, if you could walk in, you were taken.

Overseas

I complained that most of my friends had gone already overseas, and I just didn't want to stay there, and the major said, 'Well, we're going to give you first lieutenant, and you can help us.'

I said, 'I'm really not comfortable with this kind of thing.'

I think I must have been there three months and I finally headed overseas. Of course, we never knew where we were going, but we ended up in Manila and the sad thing about that is, there were about 375 of us, and we weren't welcomed. The major, who was female, came out and said that on the way over there had been nurses that had been stealing the narcotics, and there was venereal disease, and conduct certainly unbecoming an officer. That was our beginning in Manila, then we were sent to Mindoro, Philippines, and I understand Lingayen Gulf had been captured before they got to Manila, and they set up in Mindoro, it was a jungle really. I never saw anything, just the jungle and the monkeys, but they did set up an airfield, and they did that by [putting down] metal tracks, and they were able to fly the planes in and they had attacked the Japanese in Manila, but that was before I got there.

[We were at what] was called a station hospital, but it was really kind of like a lab. We had beds with mosquito netting and just canvas overhead; everything was open. We did not have any [casualties at that time] coming in from the war. We had yellow fever, we had jungle rot, we had venereal disease, we had everything like that, and malaria and dysentery. Later, much later, we were sent on to Batangas, Philippines, and right then they were beginning to get ready for the invasion of Japan. We were going to be the first ones going, but fortunately there were the two atomic bombs, and you have probably heard so many times the criticism of the atomic bombs, that the Japanese would have fought to the death and there would have been hundreds of [thousands] of Americans killed, and we knew that. So we were delighted, delighted. So many of the men had been there for about three years, and the fact that they weren't going to encounter [an invasion], that now there was a good chance they'd get back to the States, and no, I heard nothing but elation over [the bombs] and I felt the same way, but many times I heard people criticize [the decision to use them], but they were not in the war.

We still had 50,000 Japanese up in Baguio, [and their commander, General Yamashita], I guess he thought he was going to fight until the end, and the Japanese always did it that way. But they finally conquered them, and I can remember he was brought down to Manila.[12] We were still around, because we were told we could go down and visit if we wanted. I had no feeling of going down to see a man I knew would be executed, even though we had a very poor opinion of the Japanese, we now had them around the area cleaning up and they never looked at us. But [later in the United States], we also had the German prisoners, they were used in the wards, and they were having a grand time. They were trying desperately to learn English, they were wonderful.

[I returned to the States] not too long after the war. From the time we got to Fort Knox, Kentucky, there were already a lot of prisoners there. Very few Japanese, but quite a lot of the Germans

---

[12] General Yamashita-Tomoyuki Yamashita (1885-1946) was the Japanese defender of the Philippines later in the war, and he was able to hold on to part of Luzon until after the formal surrender of Japan, and afterward, he was tried for war crimes committed by his troops. It became a landmark case that affirmed the legal doctrine of command responsibility, in which a commanding officer could be held accountable for war crimes committed under his authority if he did nothing to mitigate or stop the atrocities from occurring. It is now known in international legal circles as the Yamashita standard.

that had come from the European theater. They were used in the wards, and also in the kitchens, and cleaning the area, and of course it was immaculate.

Home

There was something about the war, you didn't have to be beautiful, all you had to be was be a woman and be there. There were some romances. I myself didn't approve of them because I was afraid that in the excitement of the war, they weren't going to last, but I always did a lot of sewing and crafts, so making use of old parachutes, I rigged up a couple good [wedding dresses].

When I came back, like I said, I had my bachelor's degree, but I intended to work with a doctor and handle his clinic and I did not know the [new] medical technology part. [I used the GI Bill to] graduate with a degree in medical technology, which took me a year. I was very pleased.

[You want to know if I ever joined a veterans group?] Oh, don't start me. When I came here, I was married to a veteran who has long since died, 1973. He had been a captain and was almost called back to the Korean War again, but fortunately, he had high blood pressure and didn't get in. He had five years of [membership in a veterans group]. I said, 'Well, I want to join,' so I went over to the local [chapter].

They said, 'You cannot join as a veteran, you have to be an auxiliary.'

I said, 'Forget it!' And that was the end of that. I felt I had earned a place there, but of course, it's changed since then.

*

[How did my time in the service affect my life?] I think when I came back home, I can still remember being on that ship [coming home], I felt we had so much, so much over here and so much poverty everywhere else; of course, I had never been overseas before. And I think I'm more compassionate, I believe that in being a nurse, you have to have a lot of that. [The war did change my life], and it also made me change my thinking on a lot of things.

One soldier dead is one too many.

Katherine Denegar passed away on May 9, 2011 at the age of 94.

CHAPTER ELEVEN

The WASP

Lillian Lorraine Yonally began learning to fly at age fifteen, and at age twenty-one, became an aviation pioneer upon being accepted into another new military program for women, the Women Airforce Service Pilots. These women had to undergo the same rigorous training as their male counterparts; thirty-eight were killed in service to their country, but because at the time they were considered civilians with no military status, their fellow women classmates would often pool their money to ship the body home, with no military honors.[10] She gave this interview in 2009 at the age of 87.

Lillian Lorraine Yonally

I was born in Lynn, Massachusetts, in 1922. I moved to New Bedford, Massachusetts, and grew up there and attended school there through high school. I graduated from high school, Lincoln School in Providence, Rhode Island, a Quaker boarding school. At that point, my father remarried, because he was divorced before, and he started a second family, and I flew the coop.

Then I went to Katherine Gibbs Secretarial School in New York City. At the same time, occasionally on weekends, I took flying instructions. I finally got my private pilot license.

I [began flying] in Rochester, Massachusetts, which was actually a little field with two airplanes. I soloed there in the summer before I went to Katherine Gibbs. I think my father thought it would be a good idea for me to tackle something else, rather than see how I could drive his car. *[Laughs]*

I trained on mostly the Piper MJ-3 Cub and some Aeroncas. Both my aunt and uncle started flying at the same small airport as I did in Massachusetts. They both ended up with commercial licenses and airplanes.

So, I had a private license and was looking for a job. I got the secretarial job, which I had to stay in for six months, because that was the requirement. After that I tried Pan Am, but I did not fit in there very well. I got a job at Grumman Aircraft Engineering Corporation in Bethpage, Long Island. I was the secretary to the vice president for a while. They were building a new hangar and it was going to have a new control tower, so they needed more personnel than the two men who were doing it at that point. So they asked my boss if he would let me go, because I had a license and understood a lot about flying. I think he probably was very glad; anyway, I was! *[Laughs]* I got to go to the old control tower until the new one was built.

I was not flying on the weekends then because they closed flying on Long Island because of submarines and so forth. Everything was blacked out at night; I believe it was still before the Pearl Harbor attack. I finally bought a car—it was a Model A Ford—for thirty-five bucks and felt really special. I could now drive to Grumman instead of taking the Long Island Railroad.

I think the Pearl Harbor attack was the final blow for getting the WASPs [Women Airforce Service Pilots] going. It was so obvious that there was going to be a shortage of men flying, and they did not need them to be delivering airplanes back and forth or doing any of the other jobs they finally let us into. They started us out fairly small, but there was one group, Nancy Love's, that had pilots, some who had logged a thousand hours. They were mostly wealthy and had their own airplanes and so forth. They formed a group and worked for the ferry service.

The Women Airforce Service Pilots

The Women Airforce Service Pilots was established in August 1943. Eventually just over a thousand women were selected from over 25,000 who applied. During the war, they flew a total of 60 million miles in a host of missions.[11]

I had to be twenty-one to join. I turned twenty-one on May 5 and I had already applied for the WASP. I had a physical at Mitchell Field in Long Island by a male doctor who had never done a female, which was interesting. *[Laughs]* I passed all the way through so I was ready to go whenever they called, which was about mid-May when I got the telegram saying, 'Please show up in Sweetwater, Texas, for the seventh class.'

Training at Sweetwater, Texas

My previous boss gave me some money to work with, loaned me some money. I got a flight to Chicago, Illinois, and a flight down to Dallas, Texas, and then took the train. There were a lot of gals on the train that were coming in for that class. At Sweetwater, it was hot and dirty. It wasn't dressy, it was very casual. And it was fun with a lot of nice people.

Once we got out to the airbase, which was a couple of days later after we stayed at the hotel there for two nights, they gave us GI coveralls, the kind the mechanics wear, size forty or up! And we weren't that big. *[Laughs]* So we went back into Sweetwater and bought heavy shoes to wear, tan pants and white shirts and an overseas cap for our uniform. We found out a good system for washing them was with a scrub brush and a cake of soap. You stand in the shower, get wet, and scrub them. Then you rinse off and hang them on a hanger and in Texas they dried fairly fast; it was the only way to do it! *[Laughs]*

We had both alternating flight line and ground school. We would have flying in the morning and ground schooling in the afternoon. And then the following week we would reverse it. We started off with primary training and a PT19-A was the airplane that was low-wing with an open cockpit. It was entirely different from a Piper Cub, believe me, but great fun.

The Fairchild PT-19 was used by the USAAF during Primary Flying Training. Credit: Unknown. Licensed under CC BY-ND.

We did a lot of things I had not done before but they were explained to you and there was no problem with doing them.

[We did minimal aerobatic training]; I think the pilots liked to do that too, so we cut loops and, of course, spins. We did snap rolls and slow rolls, that kind of thing, but not anything major. The Air Force pilots, the guys, were going to do combat so they were flying in all positions. Our main thought at that time was just delivery of airplanes, to relieve them so they could do other things. At the end of primary training we had a check ride by Army personnel.

A lieutenant gave the physical training, and he yelled a lot of 'hip-hip-hop,' you know. He wasn't taking anything slowly, it had to be right, and he would call you out if you did not do it right. You were pooped when you were finished, but he wanted healthy gals. Some girls did drop out, some were excused and left. You would come back to your bay. We had six people in our long barracks, which we called bays. There were six in one room at the end, a bathroom with two stalls, and then six in the next room—that is twelve girls to a bathroom with two stalls, it kind of got busy. But you got to be very quick at things and you had to fall out into position in a marching group, squadrons with a flag. Wherever we went, we sang.

Jackie Cochran, center, with WASP trainees. Public Domain.

Jacqueline Cochran was a famous flier and a wonderful person. She was the one who started the WASPS. She was very secretive about what we did in the beginning. She did not want pictures taken. I have met her once and I'm very proud of her. She believed that girls could do this! I don't think anyone in the Army thought so. General Arnold did not think that was the place for ladies.[13] But Eleanor Roosevelt said, 'Put the girls in,' and President Franklin Roosevelt sanctioned it. It was needed, it really was. I mean there were girls flying combat in Russia, and before we were started Cochran took a group of girls over to England to fly! There were people from eight other countries who were helping fly in England, both men and women. So it was proven it could be done.

---

[13] *General Arnold-* Henry Harley "Hap" Arnold (1886-1950), then commander of the Army Air Forces.

After primary training, basic was BTs aircraft and they had a large radial engine whereas the PT19 was inlaid and they fired and made a great racket and it was entirely different.[14] They also had the blackout front section so that you could practice instruments, and that was the beginning at that point of our training, we had a great deal of learning in ground school. The worst deal of flying at that point was the radio and signals with the Morse code. I did a lot of that. Then we were checked out on instrument training— that is, flying in the front, not seeing anything, just doing it all by the needle, ball, airspeed, and a gal sat in the back, so you trusted one of the girls and she trusted you to watch, making sure you did not run into an airplane or do something silly up there. There were quite a few airplanes up there while you practiced. So you learn to trust whoever was with you and you made good friends that way.

We finished that, and the check ride by the Army, which was a sweat job, you were scared because they threw everything at you; they wanted to be sure you could do this, and I think that was wise probably. The AT-6 came next, they are used all over, they are wonderful airplanes. They will do anything. We had BTs at night, so we did night flying also.

A major part of our training was the cross-country [run]. We had to know map navigation, et cetera, because that is what they thought we would be doing, flying airplanes from the factory to the base, and returning flying deficient airplanes to the factory to be fixed and so forth. They did not know what size we would be capable of handling, but as time went on, we got more and more convinced that we could fly the bigger ones.

---

[14] *BTs* -The Vultee BT-13 was the basic trainer aircraft for American pilots during the war.

After the check ride with the AT-6s, which was much tougher because our instructor wanted that spin to come out right where he wanted it. The first one I tried did not happen that way, and I was scared.

North American AT-6C-NT Texan trainer, 1943. Credit: USAF, public domain.

He said, 'Try it again, I think you can do it,' and I did. But you were to come out on a certain heading when you do a spin. They don't teach spins, incidentally, anymore. That guy who was in Buffalo who pulled up when he should have pushed down and stalled the airplane and killed the people should have had our training or better training. You don't pull up when you are shaking, you get some air speed first.

After the AT-6 airplanes, we went to the UC-78s. We called them the 'underpowered coffins,' [the 'UC' stood for that]. It is a Cessna twin-engine, and we learned to manipulate two throttles and fly with one engine and do all of those things.

Cessna UC-78 Bobcat in flight. Used in training to bridge the gap between single and multi-engine aircraft. Source: Unknown, public domain.

The last thing we did was the night cross-country training in one of those. That was interesting. We would leave, check in, and come back. So as I said, ground school was extremely tough and a lot to face. We had Link Trainers to give us more help with night flying and blind flying.[15] When I found out you could spin in them, they went 'whoosh-whoosh!' I thought they were fun, 135ut they were very confining, and when it was hot, they were hot and sticky, though it was a good way to learn.

I got my wings in November of 1943, I had been there since May of '43. They changed as time went on, they took girls who were younger and people with less flying background training, etc. They were trying to figure out just where we fit in and how much you could ask, I think. It made a lot of sense because this was something that was new at that time.

---

[15] *Link Trainers-* flight simulators produced during the early days of aviation for U.S. military between the 1930s and 1950s by Link Aviation Devices of New York.

B-25 Training

When I graduated, twenty of us were chosen to go to Mather Field in Sacramento, California, for B-25 training. And except for one girl who found a guy she wanted to marry and quit—I can't imagine picking a guy over an airplane! — [we all went]. I mean, those B-25s were beautiful, I loved them! *[Laughs]* I stayed until I graduated with the class.

North American B-25 Mitchell. Twin engine American medium bomber, used in every theater of World War II. Source: USAF, public domain.

The B-25 makes a heck of a lot of noise. We did all kinds of special things. Colonel Wimberly was in charge of us, and he was great for that type of job. He would try new things with us and so forth. He didn't figure we had any problems at all, which was a good way to approach it, so we didn't. Of course we had ground school, engines, weather, and cross-country information training there. All kinds of stuff. We were young with open minds, a lot of room to set new things in. We did a day/night cross-country trip with two gals. This was in the winter by the way, which meant sheepskin-lined pants, jacket, helmet, boots, and heavy gloves. We always carried a flashlight with our parachute on our backs and books, so we were well loaded and strong. On this day/night cross-country trip, we went down in the daytime in Texas, just north of Mexico, then we flew back at night over the mountains so it was proof that you could do it. Two girls, no men, no one else, it was fun. It felt good.

Target Towing

Douglas SBD Dauntless; American naval scout plane and dive bomber, generally carrier based. Source: Tomás Del Coro, CC BY-SA 2.5.

When we graduated, we had a break, but I did not go anywhere. Then about half of us went to Biggs Field in Texas and the other half to March Field in Riverside, California, for the 7th Tow Target Squadron. Now I did not know what tow target was going to be. In the Mojave Desert at Camp Irwin, it was very deserty and had a lot of people working as non-coms along with our regular guys and the flight line.

Our job was to tow targets in SBDs. When you get a sleeve [a target flag trailing behind the aircraft] out back, you would fly with a tow-reel operator in the stern of the airplane. They would let the sleeve out from there when you were on course, and it would take all of the power for that SBD, having the throttle almost full forward, [because] there was a lot of drag. That was fine, we would tow the target for four hours, two two-hour shifts for the guys down below, who would be firing live ammunition at the sleeve. Each group, or battery, would dip their bullets in a different primary color. When they hit the sleeve, which was made of clear nylon material, you could read who had made hits and who did not. After the two-hour flight you would drop the sleeves as close as you could to the battery and go off and put on another sleeve for the next two hours.

This went on most of the time until the end, about December 1944. I went to Orlando, Florida, to learn how to become part of the Army Air personnel, but I did not like the idea of sitting behind a desk. When I came back from Orlando, I was shipped to Hamilton Army Airfield in San Francisco, California, where the people were returning from the island battles. [Pacific theater battles]. I did not do many things there; I could fly anything they had, and I did. I was used as a co-pilot on one flight to Mitchell Field in Long Island. Then I returned in a Grumman TBF [Avenger Torpedo Bomber] and I flew in the back of them, in the gunner's section.

Grumman TBF Avenger. Credit: U.S. Navy, 1942. Public Domain.

[The male pilots and ground personnel], they kind of avoided us, I think. Though in the officers' mess we did not have any confrontations or anything. It was generally accepted that we had qualified, and we were doing our thing. So that was good, but I did have one dispatching officer who did not like us. He gave us some bum jobs, but that was all right as long as we could do them. For example, flying a BT [Vultee-BT 13] as high as you can get it at night for searchlight training, especially on my birthday, but that is what he chose, so that is what I did. *[Laughs]* He designated what we did. Anyway, we were available for anything with any of the airplanes that we had qualified to fly.

We also did radar-tracking out of the Pacific with A-24s [Douglas A-24 Banshee Dive Bomber aircrafts], which are rather big and clumsy.[16] When you get in one of those, you don't know what you are going to be doing, but you find out before you land

---

[16] *A-24s*-Douglas A-24 Banshee Dive Bomber.

how to make it work. Three of us would go out in formation and someone in the back would drop out cut-up aluminum foil and see if they could track it from one place, and then another place. It was the beginning of radar work; that was interesting.

Then we would be sent to other fields for a week or less. We did whatever they wanted us to do with the airplane we had or what they had. It was getting more interesting for the girls because tow-target work was one thing they decided to see if we could do. We proved that we could. I think it was done with twin engines in other places, but we were given SBDs so that is what we did with them. We did have one really interesting trip with them. Three of us were asked by the head of the camp if we would come out early in the morning, before everything started, and do some diving on the troops who were in hollows between the hills; they wanted to give the troops a feeling of airplanes and so forth. We were very willing and had a great deal of fun. We stayed out for about a half hour. When I landed, the fellow who took care of my airplane said, 'Did you know that your propeller is green on the ends and your wings have green along the leading edge? And your air scoop underneath is quite green?'

I said, 'No, and I did not hurt anybody, nor hit anyone.'

He said, 'No, and you came back in good shape, but you were kind of low. Your plane has sagebrush in it!' So they did not ask us to do it again; that was too bad.

We also did what they call equiangular firing at nighttime in twin-engine aircraft, usually Beechcraft or such with two of us. This was without a horizon; it was total blackness up there, you had to use instruments. They would aim at you, but the guns would fire to the side of you. It was done with mirrors or something. So you would be flying, and these great bursts would come along side of you, so you had better focus on what you were doing.

We went into Palm Springs after that, and they had a young male cadet group, and that was kind of fun too. You could not get into March Field until about ten in the morning because of the fog, always. Flying out of there was okay going up over the mountains and into the desert, but not flying into it until after ten.

During time off, we had dates, we had a lot of things to do between us. Sharing, laundry, and all of that stuff, too. They kept us pretty busy.

Disbanded

When the WASPS were disbanded, they said, 'Thank you.' I think they said thank you, at the time I wasn't listening very closely. It was December 20 and they said to get home however you can. *[Laughs]* I wondered when they started this officer training at Air Force Strategic Air Command in Orlando if there wasn't something in the wind. I mean rumors go around all the time in the service. So when I was sent to Hamilton Field I thought, well, this is sort of a goodbye place probably. I caught a B-24 part of the way and then I don't remember what I got into, whatever I could find. I also took ground transportation and showed up on the east coast on Christmas Eve. I chose to become married with six children rather than continue, and that's okay, we all have our priorities.

I don't remember [any sort of discharge pay] or rank. I met my [future] husband when he was down on the firing line. I did not marry Jim until he came back from Korea. He had been in England, France, and Germany, through all the worst of that. After I got married, my husband did not want much to do with the WASPs and said to give my uniforms to the Salvation Army and I was a fool, I did. So I don't have a uniform, I don't think I could wear it even if I had it. *[Laughs]* I do have my wings, I had them made into a bracelet. We were the last class that was a Woman's Air Force Flying Training Detachment.

I got a job on Long Island finally. I worked for Sperry Gyroscope Company in the lab for a while testing Venturi tubes. Then I got a job as the secretary to one of the head guys and stayed there for a while. I left to get married and got a job in the Department of Aeronautical Engineering, an interesting job really and it worked out very well. They had a part of the Sperry company in Mineola, and I lived in Garden City at that point near Roosevelt Field. I bought an airplane with three guys; it had a radio in it, I'll say that for it. [Laughs] Because my family was near Cape Cod, I could fly it home on the fourth weekend, I could just go off Montauk Point. I did not have to take the Long Island Railroad; it was so much more convenient. I flew it to many other places too.

Keeping In Touch

When you go through something like that, you are really quite close. I met a lot of people that I would not have met because there would not have been this connection. We've had reunions and the last reunion was this past year. At the reunions, you see everybody and have a wonderful time. It makes you feel like you are young again!

The WASPs were not recognized for their military service until the US military began to admit the first women military pilots in the mid-1970s; it took two years of lobbying for retroactive military status to be enacted.

[We finally got our veterans status through President Carter], in 1977. It was also through Barry Goldwater and some other people who worked for us to get us that. It was a blessing because it made it possible to be a veteran and go to the Veterans Affairs for physical needs. It was something we really needed.

[My time in the WASPS definitely affected my life] a great deal. I have a very high respect for the government in flying connections; I don't think I would have been as fussy about flights going up and coming down at the right time. Yes, I am very proud of my country.

The women WASPs of World War II were finally formally honored in 2010 with the Congressional Gold Medal, sixty-six years after the Women Airforce Service Pilots was disbanded, with over 200 traveling to the US Capitol to receive the honor.

Lillian Lorraine Yonally passed away on December 31, 2021, at the age of 99.[17]

---

[17] Interested readers can view an NPR interview and slideshow of Lillian's color photographs from her service at this link: https://www.npr.org/sections/pictureshow/2010/03/a_contraband_camera_photos_of.html

CHAPTER TWELVE

The Flight Nurse

During World War II, the ranks of US military nurses expanded exponentially, from just under two thousand to nearly six thousand in the combined Army/Navy ranks. Nurses served with skill and determination in field and evacuation hospitals, and on hospital transports, including medical transport planes in the Pacific. Rose Landsman Miller served with the 809th Air Evacuation Medical Squadron in the Pacific theater. Like many, she answered the call of her country; she wanted to fly, but she became just as important as a pilot, a flight nurse ferrying wounded boys her age across the Pacific. She was a recipient of the Army Air Corps Air Medal in 1945. She sat for this interview at the end of 2009.

Rose Landsman Miller

I was born July 24, 1916, in Massena, New York. I [started] grade school in Massena and finished grade school in Syracuse. I went to Wilmington High School in Delaware for two years and finished up my high school in Massena, New York. I graduated in 1933, and I went to nurse's training in 1934 in Brooklyn, New York, in a Jewish hospital and graduated as a registered nurse in 1937. I did staffing for about a year, then I did private duty in the hospital for about three or four years before going into the service.

[When] the attack on Pearl Harbor took place, I remember I was ready to go off duty; it was about four o'clock in the afternoon and we heard this horrible news that we were at war. Now, I had had visions of flying; I had been taking flying lessons for several months. I was even taught how to land on the water, and I had to learn how to land on the land. I got as far as soloing. Everybody who flies remembers the first time they took a plane up alone. You come down, you think you were in paradise. That's the feeling that you get. I will never forget it. I learned on the Piper Cubs. Today, you get into a machine and learn everything there. Then, a number of my classmates from training were going into the service.

'I Didn't Want to Tell My Father'

I had already enlisted, in July; I didn't want to tell my father I was going into the service. You have to stop and consider, way before the draft, if someone had joined the Army at that time, [some people got the idea that there was] something wrong with them. It was almost like they [must have been] the dregs of society. So my father always had an idea that the service was something else, and I was very reluctant to tell him. But my oath had already been in, and when my orders came home that's when I told him. I think by that time he kind of accepted that this was war. I guess he was very proud of the fact that I was the only one in the whole family that was able to put my time and energy into helping people. My brother could not go for physical reasons and the rest of us were all women. I had gone down, and I applied, but we had to go through the Red Cross; at that time, nurses had to go through the Red Cross. We were not considered part of the service. It was all complicated. But once we were in the service, we were given the rank of first lieutenant.

We were sent to Atlantic City; Atlantic City at that time was an air base. There, we encountered everything that was thrown at us. I'll use that word. We weren't receiving any wounded at that time, it was just an enlisted base. We were issued white uniforms, white caps, and shoes. We encountered meningitis there. In fact, [in one instance when I was there], the base was almost closed to anybody coming in or going out, even by train. I would say because we were alerted and knew about a lot of these things, we saved an awful lot of these boys. I know that there were over five of them we could not save. That was unfortunate. We just couldn't, and that was it.

One time, at lunchtime, all the officers would go to lunch and leave [one of us] on. When I was there, they were ready to admit a patient with a temperature, and I loosened his coat. I took a look and said, 'You have a stiff neck.'

I saw these marks on his neck and called down to the admitting office and said, 'I'm not admitting him to a pneumonia ward. I am sending him upstairs to the meningitis ward.' That's how quickly we saved all the rest of them—that we knew.

Well, things changed, and spring came, everything was fine again. Then in April or May, there were two of us who had applied for flight training. I was a little bit annoyed [when she was tapped for the program before me, having had earlier flight training], because I said, 'Why did they call her before me?'

Anyway, I knew a number of the officers, and they said, 'Well don't worry about it because you're gonna be in the next class.' Turns out they had to take her because of her age; if they didn't call her, she was going to be over the age of going [next time].

So I was in the next class, and they sent me to Bowman Field for flight training. We had to adapt how to conduct ourselves in the plane. They were all mockups like the C-40, we'd go in with equipment and come out with patients. In the interim, once the equipment was unloaded, they had to set up what is called a litter strap. The litters were just slipped into the litter straps. We had to learn all these things in order to do our jobs.

'We Didn't Know Where We Were Going'

In the meantime, they sent us to different hospitals to do this and that. Around November, they had already broken up our class and put us into our squadrons. The squadrons consisted of twenty-five nurses. There were four flights of six nurses, plus the chief nurse. Around the end of October, our squadron was called to attention, and [the commander] said, 'The first group of you will be leaving in four hours to San Francisco.' So that meant packing up quickly and getting everything ready to leave in four hours! We got down to the plane; they bumped everybody else off. They broke us up so that each group went onto a different plane, and we all met in San Francisco. We didn't know where we were going.

When we got to San Francisco, they equipped us with arctic gear boots, parkas, you name it! Around the first week of November, we were alerted for our next flight. We were leaving on four C-54s, they weren't passenger planes. They were these big C-54s and they were able to fly long distances. Three of us left on time, and one was a little delayed because of engine problems. We got there on a Friday. The plane that got left behind, one of the nurse's husbands was based at Wheeler Field with the fighter planes.

She said to the chief nurse, 'Would you please call when you get there and tell Ray I'm coming down.'

So she called the commanding officer when we landed and he said, 'When she comes in, have her call me.'

Well, Sunday morning their plane landed, and she called the commanding officer and he said, "You stay right there, I'm sending him down to get you!'

The husband was probably a first lieutenant at that time and he's fussing and fuming, 'Why should I go down and pick up a lousy second lieutenant?' He doesn't know who this is, you know. The crew was alerted when they landed, and the crew disappeared as he was about to pick her up. When she got out of the car, her husband said to her, 'Annie, what are you doing here? Go on home!' [Laughs]

Anyway, like I said, it took us close to four or five months before Admiral Nimitz decided that flight nurses were okay in the Pacific, because he had said there's no place for them here. Well, I would like to say we proved him wrong.

The first group was sent down to Port Moresby to evacuate anybody coming up. They were to bring all the injured all the way up to Hickam Field, which would have been over thirty hours. There would be two nurses coming up alone only with their crew and their patients. When they finally got up, they decided it was too much. I mean you can't put someone on a plane and ask them to take care of their patients for thirty-six hours all alone. So they decided no, they broke that up, so then they were going from Port Moresby, New Guinea, into Guadalcanal. From Guadalcanal they would go into Kanton Island, then back to Hickam Field [Army Air Base, Oahu, Hawaii].[18] Then another flight would be taking the States runs, which would have been anywhere from twelve to fourteen hours, depending on the winds. Finally, they sent the second group down to Guadalcanal and that was going to be al-

---

[18] *Kanton Island-* Coral atoll in Kiribati in the Central Pacific. Tarawa is the capital of Kiribati.

most twenty hours in the air. The third group would be taking them to the States and the fourth group was going on to Tarawa.

I remember the first flight, we hadn't really begun our runs [but] then suddenly they said, 'The two of you will be going to Kanton Island to pick up five burn cases.'

You see, a plane had hit a bunker and blew up, and five of them were burned, so they sent us down to bring them back. When we got down there—that's almost nine to ten hours down and nine to ten hours back—the patients were just swathed completely. The treatment that they got down in Kanton Island must have been so good that when we met one of them, all he had was just a little scar on his nose. The treatment that we were getting in the Pacific was unbelievable.

'This One Needs Me'

From that time on [we were assigned to] the four spots. I was down on the Guadalcanal run and I picked up a flight there, that one had just come out of New Guinea.

[An officer] said, 'I think you had better prepare a blood transfusion when you get to Kanton Island.'

'Why?' You see, this was sixty-five years ago, and everything was different then.

'He has aplastic anemia.' Now that could have been anything, he probably could have had leukemia, or whatever. The poor boy was oozing blood from his mouth, all he was doing was spitting. So before we took off, I wired ahead for whole blood transfusion. So for nine hours from when we took off I strapped on the oxygen, all we had was a little tank. No sooner did I have it on, he said, 'I have to spit.' Off comes the mask, put it back on, 'I have to spit.' You fly with one nurse and one corpsman for about thirty-five patients. So I said to my corpsman, 'You look after all these others, this one needs me.'

So for the rest of the flight I took the mask on, off. On, off, you know what I mean? We landed on Kanton Island, they took him off and they gave him a transfusion.

As soon as the transfusion was over, he was loaded back up. We took off and it was fine, I could strap the mask on and attend to the other ones. When we landed at Hickam Field, I told my commanding officer I would suggest that this boy remain on the ground and have him transfused before going out on the next leg of the flight. He said, 'I'm sorry but he's going out in about four hours.' Well, he was the commanding officer, there was nothing else I could do, but let me put it this way, if it had been one of the other girls, the southern girls, he would have listened. This commanding officer was a southerner from maybe Mobile, Alabama. [Laughs] I had two strikes against me, he didn't like me—firstly, I was a damn Yankee, and secondly, I was Jewish, so he didn't like me, period. Anyway, the boy went out four hours later and they almost lost him. My roommate was on that plane and she said they almost lost him—the only thing they had [onboard] was plasma. To this day I only hope he was able to get home before he went.

'A Planeload of Psychos'

He wasn't a war wounds patient, but we evacuated everything from war wounds to psychos, to medical problems and whatever. We also evacuated more psychos and more jungle rot. If it wasn't our turn to go out, we would have had a little clinic and we would bring our patients in there for a few hours. While I was there, they brought some of these jungle rots in, and the stench was overpowering. Now how the girls sat there for eight hours and smelled that, I really don't know. We never knew what we were picking up. Over the years, you remember the bad ones. You re-member the psychos. For every planeload of patients we were bringing out of the South Pacific, we had to have five psychos on the plane. They tried bringing out a planeload of psychos one time and it didn't work.

Anyway, on one of my planes we had a latrine, and one of these patients decided to get up and streak up and down the plane. *[Laughs]* Like I said, you look at it and see a bit of humor in spite of the war. There was one psycho case who saw ducks, he was in New Guinea, wherever he went he saw ducks. Well, the psychia-trist tried to rid him of the ducks. Finally, they sent him back but he still saw his ducks. They decided, he's no good, we'll send him back to the States as a Section 8. Well, it's four hours from New Guinea to Guadalcanal, another twenty hours to Hickam Field, another fourteen hours to San Francisco. All of this time he saw his ducks. Finally, about an hour out from San Francisco he calls the flight nurse over and said, 'Lieutenant, you can have the ducks now, I don't need them anymore.' *[Laughs]*

Later I was on the Kwajalein run. From Kwajalein we went off to Saipan and Guam. When hospital ships picked up the wounded in Saipan, they unloaded 1,500 sick and wounded at Kwajalein. We had all of those sick and wounded back in Hawaii in the gen-eral hospitals in less than a week. Where if the hospital ship had gone, it would have taken them three weeks out and then three weeks back. I guess we proved Nimitz wrong.

My last flight, we went from Kwajalein into Guam and Saipan. I think it was in Saipan that they gave us the quarters just beyond the hospital so that we wouldn't interfere with the nurses and all; [I was at Saipan right after the bonzai attack.] The Japanese that were still there did not want to be taken by the Americans. Whether they were afraid or whatever, I don't know. All the fami-lies committed suicide. There was a section there called Suicide

Cliff.[19] They would line up their children and push them off the cliff! Then the second one would push the other until the father was left and then he would jump. These were high cliffs, so you can just imagine. They also had a lot of sugar cane factories there and it was a very peculiar smell, very unpleasant. Most of us were pretty close to the air base so it didn't bother us that much.

'We Flew the Entire Pacific'

People used to say, weren't you afraid of flying that whole distance with nothing in between? We said no, it never occurred to us. There was a plane going from Hickam Field to Saipan and the

---

[19] *Suicide Cliff*-She most likely refers to Marpi Point. One veteran in Volume 8 remembered: 'At the end of the battle, [I witnessed] the most eerie, bizarre thing that I ever saw in my life. Up at the end there was a place called Marpi Point. We were there for two or three days, just watching people commit suicide, civilians basically jumping into the water, blowing themselves up with grenades, having their own soldiers shoot them.

What had happened was the end of the island was covered with a shrubbery very tight, like a hedge. It was also coral, and it was pockmarked with these holes, so people could get in these holes all along there. Then there was a cliff just about a thousand feet from the edge, which had caves in the underside. There was a path going down into the flatland before you got into the water.

There were some Japanese soldiers apparently up in the cave underneath where we were standing. A lot of other people were hidden in these caves all along. But they had gotten the people afraid of us, probably terrified of [us] coming. So, we went down there, we sent scouts down there [first]. A couple of them got killed by the snipers, so we pulled back to the cliff line and then had the Japanese speakers try to convince the people that we weren't going to harm them. But I would imagine [they were] like, 'Who are they kidding?' There was nothing much we could do at that point. The killing just started. I saw whole families standing on a rock, right along the ocean, and explode a grenade, and then maybe a survivor would crawl off into that water. [But as an eighteen or nineteen-year-old in combat], I think by that time, I was a little deadened about anything shocking me. I thought much more about it in years after.'

plane went down. What happened, no one will ever know. They never found [them]. And yet, we flew the entire Pacific.

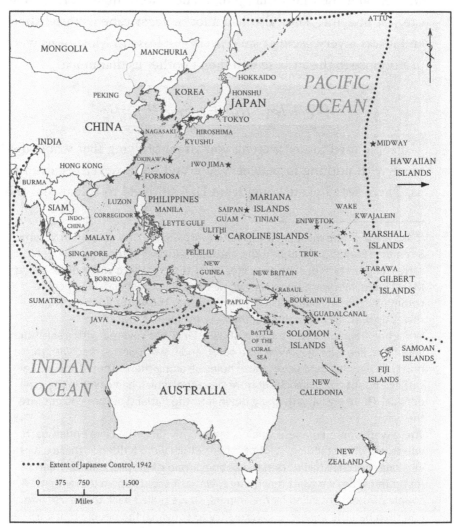

The vastness of the Pacific Theater. Extent of Japanese control, 1942. Drafted by Susan Winchell, after Donald L. Miller.

Yes, many times we came in on three engines and hoped to God we didn't feather another one. Now, coming into San Francisco in the middle of winter, the fog hangs over there like pea soup. You can't see in front of you. We had no radar then. There were four airfields that we could use; you never knew where you were going to land. One plane came in and it was all fogged out; [the pilot radioed that] he's going over the mountains. I guess they tried to reach Reno, but they had to land on a fighter training strip because they were running out of fuel. We came in once, again practically closed in with fog and cloud cover, and our pilot said, 'I'm going to try Oakland!', and so help me God, he found a hole in the clouds and came down in Oakland. We just would never know. We could be losing fuel or hitting a mountain, because all along the coast are mountains. And yet, I guess our faith in our pilots was such that we didn't really think about it; it's a job to be done, and that's it.

People would say to me, 'What did you see when you were over there?' I said, "See? Sky, water, and telephone poles!' They would say, 'Telephone poles?' 'Yes, when you bomb an island, what do you think is left standing? Telephone poles!' [Laughs]

On Guadalcanal, New Guinea, Saipan, Guam, and Tinian, nurses were quartered behind fences and guarded and escorted to their hospitals and activities by MPs. They were subject to evening curfews and armed escorts after 1800 hours. Women's Army Corps (WAC) members here received the same treatment. Women were restricted ostensibly to protect them from the Japanese, but in reality, it was to cut down on incidents of sexual intimidation or harassment, and fraternization.[12] MacArthur's orders fooled no one.

Nurses relaxing, Guam. Donald P. Quarters collection.
Courtesy Jackie Quarters.

In between our flights, it might have seemed we had a lot of time off because for every twelve hours in the air you had to be on the ground a full two days. They had one flight down in the South Pacific doing the New Guinea to Guadalcanal run, which was four hours in and four hours back with your patients, which was eight hours in the air. Then another twenty-eight hours to Hickam Field. If they didn't have enough of their nurses, they would pull ours. That meant these girls were in the air twenty-eight hours. We would come off like this *[shakes both her hands in a nervous gesture]*. We couldn't eat, we couldn't sleep. At one time we were all taking Seconal to help us sleep. Even that didn't work, so they issued a command that we had to be on the ground for at least for-

THE THINGS OUR FATHERS SAW (VOL. IX) | 157

ty-eight hours. There was one ground nurse who had to be flown out somewhere and when she got off, she said, 'I would not want your job!' We were considered the elite. We were different, you know. Now, it doesn't make any difference. When you take a look at the equipment on the plane that we had, you would not believe how primitive it was. We had no penicillin at that time.[20] We had sulfur, sedatives, and pain killers. But there were a lot of things we just did not have. Sometimes you wonder how in the world we ever won the war *[Laughs]*. We had used up a year's supply of aspirin in six months. At one time in the hospital, we had about 1,500 patients of various conditions, they had no urinals. So what do you do? You need the urinals. They went to the Red Cross, who brought back all types of shapes and sizes of vases to use as urinals. *[Laughs]*. That's why I said, how we won the war, I don't know. It was just persistence, I guess.

Olivia De Havilland and Betty Grable

We saw an awful lot of USO shows. But most of the time when we were there, we didn't have very much time to sit in on them, because we were either coming or going. I was coming up from Guadalcanal, we were on Kanton Island, and we heard a VIP was coming down. Everybody was saying who's this VIP? It could have been a general. The plane landed and what came off the plane was a lady. Have you ever heard of Olivia De Havilland? She was beautiful. But more than beautiful, she was a lady. She came off the

---

[20] *We had no penicillin at that time-* While penicillin production was being ramped up, especially in the buildup to the June 1944 Normandy campaign, it was also in short supply. It was not until June 1945 that large-scale mass production enabled by the War Production Board was reaching its peak. Source: Parascandola, J. *The History of antibiotics: a symposium.* American Institute of the History of Pharmacy No. 5. 1980.

plane in a simple dress, normal high heels, but gracious. I'm a woman and I look at her and just say, 'Oh!' The aura that she expelled was like the essence of womanhood. She wasn't Betty Grable, excuse me, [laughs] but like I said, she was a lady. She could have been your sweetheart, your wife, your mother, your sister, everything. I mean, that is the way I looked at her and I think the men looked at her the same way.

Betty Grable was, I'll use the word, a bore. There was an occasion in the South Pacific with the USO troupe, and Betty Grable was there. She happened to ask one of the flight nurses if they could iron her costume for her. I hate to tell you what they told her to do. [Laughs]. The idea is that we're working our necks off and she's enjoying herself, I'll use that word. Oh well.

The Philippines

We never experienced a bombing, but once when we went into Okinawa, we went in on red alert. Anything could have happened, a bomb or an airplane could have come over and hit the airfield. We were down there for only two hours, enough to load up our patients, refuel, and get the hell out of there. When we went into the Philippines [in 1945], my husband and I were on our honeymoon; we had a week to ten days of R&R. That's the time that they went and evacuated all of the internees [of the Japanese, from the conquest in 1942]. They said these girls, these nurses, were coming out almost like skeletons. For three years they were interned.

One of the stories that came out of the Philippines was about a Japanese soldier who had appendicitis and had to get his appendix out. So they made sure the American doctors and nurses took care of that. They were standing over them with guns. Fortunately, he recovered, and because of that they got an extra ration of rice or something. So there were all kinds of stories that came out.[21] One of these days I will get that book about these nurses that got caught in the Philippines. Now as far as MacArthur is concerned, we did not like him, period. He was a very selfish man. Instead of trying to get some of the other Americans out, he loaded up his plane with his household goods, things like that.[22] The people who were down in the Philippines, who got captured and even after we went in, they did not like him, period. You read the history books and you think, well that didn't happen like that. History actually distorts reality. I suppose that's the way it is.

Tarawa

When we were on Tarawa, the Navy had no idea how to set up a ground facility. Two of our girls came down with dysentery and they were isolated for about six weeks. Like I said, the facility wasn't the cleanest and that was the Navy. Maybe it's different today, but it wasn't then.

Sometimes we were housed in a Quonset hut, but sometimes it was just a wooden shack to keep the rain off. That was just about it. When you were down in Tarawa, it was just a small wooden building. The water was brackish. If we wanted to go out and bathe in the ocean, we wanted to be sure the squids weren't there.

---

[21] "In February 1945 U.S. troops liberated the sixty-seven Army nurses who had been imprisoned in Santo Tomas Internment Camp since 1942 and evacuated them to a convalescent hospital on Leyte. Although suffering from malnutrition and beriberi, they recovered from their ordeal fairly quickly. The duty they performed in combat and the hardships they endured as prisoners of war are testaments to the professionalism of the entire Army Nurse Corps throughout the war." Source: *The Army Nurse Corps in World War II*. U.S. Army Center of Military History, p. 30.

[22] *he loaded up his plane with his household goods* -General Douglas MacArthur and his family, ordered by the President to leave, were evacuated from Corregidor in a risky PT boat operation in March 1942.

There was a little ledge, and very often they would be hiding under there. Not too bad, but you had to be careful. On Kanton Island, there were two coconut trees and some desert bushes and that's it. A number of our girls were fair-skinned; fortunately my skin is not fair. But if they went from our quarters, which is about from here to that chair [*gestures across room*], they would be burned. A lot of the girls came down with bad sunburns. Me, I just turned so dark; my daughter has a picture somewhere in which I look like one of the natives. Yet when I got back, all I did was this [*rubbing her forearm*]; I didn't burn, fortunately; I just flaked off a little bit.

Food

[In the mess hall, we had] Vienna sausages, pancakes, and anything that was canned, powdered eggs. When we went to the States and back, we would pick up the things we didn't have before. I remember once we had strawberries or something and we would come back, and we would share it. For some reason or other we couldn't get very much chicken, so we would bring that back from the States, the makings for dinner. In Hawaii, we would get fresh fruit, but wherever else we were, we didn't get it. If we were on Kwajalein, there was nothing there but coconuts, Guam and Saipan [also]. Everything was being brought in by ship. Everything was canned, the fruit, vegetables, everything like that. I think 'oleo' got started there too. We had heard something about a substitute for butter, we didn't know what it was, but it was used. Today, it was probably a form of oleo. When you get home, you want all the things you didn't have before. You want to go out for dinner and get a good steak. Or you want something fancy that you hadn't had in years. So in a way, you begin to enjoy yourself.

Marriage

I met my [future] husband at Hickam Field. I was in the [Army] Air Force and he was in the Signal Corps, in the ground force. One time he was telling me they had to set up communications in Kauai. Now Kauai is a peculiar island, I'll say it that way, because you can't go all the way around the island because the mountains go right through to the end all the way down. You have to use a boat to go all the way around. They had to set up communications right through the mountains, through the forest, all the way through. They had to set up communications in Hawaii on top of the mountains. That was his job.

Of course, like everything else, you're on Hickam Field base and you get to know all the officers there.

I had gotten quite friendly with the general next door; he would send his orderly in and invite me to dinner. I complained to him that my husband could not get off the island at all. He said, 'Don't worry about it. You set up the time you want to get married and I'm sure he'll be there.' Anyway, we didn't know when the war was going to be over. I had already been overseas eighteen months and he had been overseas longer than that. The next thing I knew, I got a letter from my husband setting up the time that he would be there! I guess it's important that you get to know different people.

We were married in February 1945, by the chaplain from Pearl Harbor. The chaplain was from the Navy, a little Chinese boy played the organ, a Marine sang the hymns. So, it was kind of an international wedding. At that time, you couldn't be married and be on the same base. We were talking about it [beforehand] and decided that if we got married and went back to the States, I'd be on one end, and he'd be on the other. So, we decided I'll get out of the service. I'll get pregnant.

*

My last flight was to Okinawa. I was getting morning sickness, and it was a little bit too much. I just turned myself in to the Medical Department and was discharged in San Francisco in June, but it didn't take effect until August. I should have waited a little bit longer because in August they dropped the bomb and that was it.

After that, I went to my husband's folks. They were waiting for me; they had only met me once in San Francisco. My father-in-law was a theatrical lawyer, and he had some business out there. My mother-in-law came out first. I met them both in Los Angeles. They were very anxious for me to come back; they had heard I became pregnant. I stayed with them. I went back to Massena for a while to see my folks. We couldn't even find housing; at that time, even after the war was over, there was no housing available. If you had a room in a house, you were lucky. Nothing was available until the new housing developments went up.

In September, my husband was discharged, right after the war ended. There was something very funny. We went to a party, by this time I was about eight months pregnant. There was a fella there who asked, 'When did your husband get back?'

I said September, and here I am like this. [*Holds hands out in front, showing pregnancy*]. He looks at me, and his face dropped!

I said, 'Oh, I forgot to tell you, we were married overseas!' [*Laughs*]

[When my husband was discharged, he made use of the G.I. Bill], he went back to law school. He was supposed to have joined his father in the law business, but like everything else, a lot of things fell apart. His father died, and like I told you, things fell apart. By that time, I had the one child and then fifteen months later my daughter was born. So with him going to school it was impossible for me to go back to school. I just went back to nursing. At one point someone had asked me, when you went back to work, how did the other nurses treat you? I couldn't understand what she meant. Then I began to understand what she meant, because I didn't go back to work until seven or eight years later. By that time, the war was over and I said, 'They treat you like any other nurse.' They didn't ask you where you were or anything else.

The World War II Flight Nurses Association

About four or five years after the war, the flight nurses decided they were going to have their own group. There were 1,500 flight nurses worldwide. We covered everything from North Africa, all of Europe, England, the CBI (China, Burma, India) route; the girls flying that route, they were flying the Hump, [the eastern end of the Himalayan Mountains]. And of course, we flew the entire South Pacific. Because there weren't that many of us, when you compare the 1,500 of us to those [thousands] of nurses on the ground, we weren't very many. So we decided to form the World War II Flight Nurses Association. We more or less once a year have a reunion, but since we are losing more every year, it has dwindled down. If we have one hundred fifty nurses in a year, that's an awful lot. In January we hope to have the last reunion, I hope it isn't. There's a lot that I know we have lost contact with completely, and we know those that have gone, but outside of that, we don't know where a lot of them are. And that was it.

*

'Leave Me Alone'

It's difficult to say [how the war affected my life] because once you come back and you pick up ordinary life again, it's almost like a bad dream—or a good dream you had, depending how you look at it. I really don't know, [but I had no trouble adjusting to civilian life].

When I first got back, my mother-in-law asked me if I wanted to go to the Congregational church meeting? I said, 'No, I am very happy just sitting here.'

Nobody's going to tell me when to get up, nobody is going to tell me when to go to bed. Nobody's going to tell me when to go out. Just let me sit for a while. That's the way I felt. Leave me alone.

Less than four percent of American soldiers who received medical care in World War II were lost. Just forty-six of the nearly 1.2 million patients flight-evacuated during the war did not survive. This is a testament to the professionalism and standards that our nurses created, and lived by.[13]

Rose L. Miller was honored as the grand marshal of her hometown's Memorial Day parade in 2012. She passed at the age of 96 the following November.

CHAPTER THIRTEEN

The WAVE

Margaret Doris Alund-Lear was a 1942 graduate of Catholic Central High School in Troy, New York. In 1943, she joined the US Navy WAVES training program at Hunter College in the Bronx and then was posted to Washington, D.C. at the Naval Air Station in Anacostia, preparing flight maps for pilots. Later, she was chosen to participate at the famous Sixth War Loan Drive in Chicago, which brought 600,000 people a day to the Navy Pier to meet the famous movie personalities and view the latest equipment the Navy was using. Later, she was assigned back to Washington at the largest WAVES station, with 5,000 women serving there. She was a chaplain's assistant, visiting the hospitals for the sick and wounded in the war.

Margaret Doris Alund-Lear

I was born in Watervliet, New York, on September 21, 1923. I went to Catholic Central High School. I majored in business, but I studied drama and art. I did a lot of public speaking and was in various plays and things in school.

[The attack on Pearl Harbor] was such a shock at the time to all the seniors. Everyone seemed to want to do something. What can we do? I remember talking about it and then my brothers went into the service, one in the Army and one in the Navy. I was very close to my brothers, and it was quite a loss without them at home. That was when I saw pictures of women and I thought, this is for me. I'm going! I really felt that I wanted to do something. I was working in the telephone company, and I said no—I want to leave and go into the service. And my girl chum was going to go with me. We were to meet the next day; I showed up, and she didn't. I enlisted in Troy, New York, the third week in March 1944.

The WAVES

I went into the WAVES when they were new to the country.[23] That was for me, I was really excited about it. My parents, of course, said, 'Well now, a third one going, but we can't stop you.' I said, 'No, you can't.' I had never been to a big city, but I had my orders and went down. I was amazed at New York City and had to go to a center where they did all the health checkups and everything. I came back home, and they told me I was leaving for the boot camp training at Hunter College in the bronx. So here was a little girl from a small town going down by various means on subways and so forth to get around New York City. But it was exciting, and I really felt I was getting somewhere at that point.

My active duty began April 6. I had six weeks of boot camp at Hunter College. The day we arrived, we received all of our clothing and the next morning at six we had to march to breakfast. The marching was new, the clothing was new. We had cotton stockings because of the war. And to a woman who loved nylons, that was something different to wear! The cotton stockings were

---

[23] *WAVES*- Women Accepted for Volunteer Emergency Service/US Navy Women's Reserve, established on July 30, 1942 to free up men for sea duty.

heavy, believe me. The short, flat oxford shoes were different also, but we found out we needed the oxfords because of all the marching. They gave us a song sheet and we had to sing on the way to breakfast. Then they informed us there was such a thing as 'captain's inspection.' So we girls had to learn how to have everything in the drawers a certain way, and everything had to hang a certain way. And in between times we were so busy marching, and there was so much to learn. For example, we never knew about certain ships and Link Trainers and all these different things. So we had to learn as the men learned about the Navy and the chain of command.

Another thing we learned was we could no longer decide what we were going to do, we were told what we were going to do for six weeks. It was wonderful training and we shaped up. I enjoyed that. Waiting for our billet [postings], we had a graduation ceremony in one of the huge armories down there. The experience was very exciting, [leaving me] to swell with pride, believe me. When you were marching and doing it right, that took six weeks to be perfect, but we were perfect! The other thing was the people in the Bronx would watch us marching. They would be so excited, to see these women learning how to conform. Then we had our shipping orders, we were all going to various places. We had our picture taken all together, we had a lot of camaraderie. It was very, very good. We did a lot of studying and took tests. I would like to say that I ran a switchboard in the telephone company, but I never had to do one in the Navy.

WAVE Quarters One

My first billet was Washington, D.C.; when we got there, that was a shock. It was so beautiful! We were sent to WAVE Quarters I, which was on the Potomac River. We could see the Jefferson

Memorial and the Washington Monument; it was just breathtaking. We had three airports that formed a 'V', and all the military planes were coming and going all the time.

Believe me, for a sailor woman, it was inspiring at the time. At WAVE Quarters I, they said, 'Well, we don't know yet what we are going to do with you. Everyone serves a mess detail in the Navy, so until we get you a billet, we are going to have you in ship's company and you will have to do a mess detail.'

We would feed two thousand a meal, and they kept coming from all over, officers and enlisted men as well. After each meal, we would have to clean the floor. I had never scrubbed floors and we had large, large mops. You had to squeeze the mops out, and the floors in our mess hall were wooden. We would also have to perfectly line up the salt and pepper shakers with a string on all these long tables. I had to take care of the coffee urn, which meant I had to climb up onto a bar and get down into it with steel wool. You had to keep going over it with your hands so that there was no residual coffee marks on it. I was down into it practically to my head to clean it. All the [large pans that the food was in] also had to be cleaned. Then the officer would come and check everything afterward; we made sure they were cleaned. You wondered, is that what I'm going to do? But you took it, you didn't complain.

We had to wear jeans; I had never worn dungarees. But that was the Navy, you wore the shirts and the dungarees. I [also] had to pluck chickens, I was so sick plucking chickens that I thought I was going to faint one time! [Laughs] They said, 'Well, we will take you off the chickens. You are doing good on the cleaning!' We used to go back to the barracks and laugh and say, 'Look what we are doing!' But it was interesting.

Mapwork

After the ship's company, they said, 'You are going to be down at the Naval Air Station. You are going to paint maps. We understand you took art.'

'Yes, I used an airbrush.'

They added, 'But understand, it is going to be secret. You cannot tell anyone what you are doing. You cannot tell your parents; you are not to talk about the work. You will be there, but you won't talk to anyone, and you will be inspected every day.'

So we would carry our purses, we wouldn't take any junk in them. They inspected us as we went in and when we came out. We sat at long tables, you could see the maps in the room, whatever they were made with, big white things that they would spray green. Then we would see all these designs that we had to put the roads, the pillboxes and the hills in. We had everything to do on these maps. We were painting them all the time, some of them with an airbrush, others with the tiniest of brushes, to paint everything perfectly. A steady hand was needed; I was able to do it, and I enjoyed it. But you would see the other women working but you did not talk to them. You kept your mind on your work. There were large and small maps. Some of the large ones I had never seen until I watched a history program. I got so excited one day, I said, 'There is my map!' and my husband said, 'You finally saw one.' I said, 'Yes, that is what we were doing!' It was only after the war when they told us we could discuss the maps that we had painted. It was kind of hard not being able to tell your parents what you did.

Oh, we worked all day. We would get there at eight in the morning and then at four o'clock the bus would come. We would go outside, get inspected again, and then be taken back to the barracks. It was very interesting; I did that for roughly four months.

Celebrity Bond Drive

Then the commander said, 'You have been chosen to go to Chicago. They are having the biggest bond drive of the war, and you will be a representative of New York State.' I said what do I do, sell bonds? She said, 'You will do everything. The commander there will be your boss. You will follow him around and do whatever he wants you to do. You will greet the people coming in, hand out programs, familiarize yourself with the area so you can talk about it. They are going to sell bonds and will have all the radio and movie people there. The Admiral is coming, everyone is coming to see the new equipment we are going to use in this war!' When they said you are going to see a lot of people, well, I didn't realize I was going to see 500,000 people all in a group! [The *Chicago Sun* newspaper with the headline '*Navy Bond Show Attracts 500,000*' is displayed. It was all day long, but it was an honor. It was wonderful, they put us up in The Drake Hotel, which is a gorgeous hotel. They had given it over to the war effort, so it was all military people, and it was beautiful. We met so many people there, I can remember a baseball team [owner] and he was quite famous. I met Gloria Vanderbilt's husband at the time, his name was Pat DiCicco. He was a very interesting man. I also saw Judy Garland and Eddie Cantor, Dorothy Lamour and Red Skelton, he was wonderful. So many movie stars, we would escort them to the stage, and they would do their bits; it was very, very nice.

After us girls did our duty, we would walk down to Chicago. I remember seeing the Christmas tree at Marshall Fields. One of the girls told me to meet her and we would have lunch. I did not know they had seven cafeterias in the place so you can imagine my feelings about trying to find her! I was a lost country girl, but it was a wonderful experience to meet all of these people. I was right at home with them, everybody was so nice to me, it was very exciting. I have pictures of the girls from the tour; when I came back from the tour, I was so exhilarated. I thought the experience was so grand, I thought, 'I don't know what I'm going to do now!'

They said, 'Well, we have a new job for you. You are going to WAVE Quarters D in Washington, D.C., [the largest, state-of-the-art training facility]. Well I loved WAVE Quarters I, which was new, Quarters D was an older one.

'You are going to be a chaplain's assistant. You can be a yeoman striker,' [administrative position], which takes a year to do it. Commander Tom Fallon was going to be my boss. He was a very nice Irish priest and very direct to the point when he wanted something. He would say, 'Get this off!', and then I would have to get a letter off to this or that person. He had been on a battleship, and he was very interesting. He told me about all the people on the ship when it was hit. He had brought a lot of rosaries with him, but he said even those who were not Catholic wanted rosaries. The fellows were really scared; that battleship was being bombed, and many sailors were badly hurt. He was a very dedicated man who would do everything for the men.

He started retreats and brought Monsignor Fulton Sheen to speak.[24] I would like to say, Fulton Sheen was remarkable. We arranged for a retreat and had the lights off. Monsignor Sheen came down the aisle then onto the stage looking down on the audience; he scared the daylights out of us. He said loudly, 'Where are you going?'

We all said, 'What did we do?', but he was such a wonderful speaker with penetrating eyes. He came several times just to see us! What a remarkable man; if you did not have some kind of

---

[24] Fulton J. Sheen (1895 -1979) was a Catholic bishop of the Catholic Church highly regarded for his work in television and radio.

faith, he would give it to you. He would make you feel that you better get to church once in a while or something.

The Flag

Every day in our place, we had to have the flag ceremony. I was part of the ship's company, so we would have to go out and march; all of the WAVES would march out and raise the flag. I think today, since 9/11 when people see the flag, they are getting the feeling that I, and many of us in the service, had. We all stopped. If you were on the street, all the cars around the Communication Annex where I worked all stopped until that flag got up. It was something, to look around and see this happening. The cars, kids going to work, and we ourselves being in it, it was very exciting. Then, at eight o'clock at night, it would come down. To this day when I see a parade, people look at me because I am saluting. I feel so deeply about the country and the flag means something.

I was only twenty years old, and it was just grand to grow up like that and know what life was about. I also did a lot of writing. I had to answer letters regarding girls that were going to be married or the young men from Communications across the street. We had to get all their records so they could get married. The chaplain would take me to Bethesda Hospital, it was one of the biggest hospitals I had ever seen. It would make Albany Medical look small. If people want to see what war is, they should go in the hospital. Some men had no faces, no legs, no arms. I saw so much, to this day, I still think about it. I did see them all doing little things to keep busy. What the chaplain said was, 'You'll notice some of the men are walking around with toilet paper. Everybody in the Navy that can walk does a job. It restores their dignity and lets them think they can do something.'

I can remember the chaplain saying, 'You girls go out with all the young, good-looking fellas, but how about taking some of these guys out?' So we started saying, 'Would you like to go to lunch with us?' Cabs were cheap then, thirty-five cents for a whole zone in Washington. The boys would say, 'I would love to go out!' I have a picture of a young man that I took out, he had only one leg. My girlfriend was going with her boyfriend who had come home, and we took this young man with us, it was my last night in Washington. I had been married the month before and I called my husband. I said, 'I'm going to take a young man out.'

He said, 'Do it!' I just felt that I should let my new husband know that I was going out with someone. [Laughs] It was quite an experience to work for the chaplain and see all these things.

To me, to this day, I feel I would have gone now if my country needed me. I believe America is a wonderful country. I've been to Europe, and I have seen people are not as fortunate to work, like we could work and have the things we have here. I'm very dedicated to this country.

A Cosmopolitan Wedding

Oh, I have to tell you about my wedding! I had a plumber that used to come in and out fixing things. Even if our typewriter broke, he would fix that, he could do anything. When I was going to be married, he said, 'I would like to see you get married.' I said yes. I also had two African American women that were maids. In Washington, in the days of segregation, when you went down to Thirteenth Street, they had barricades. You could not go over there. The two girls that cleaned the office were so lovely to me, I got along with everybody. They said, 'We are coming to your wedding.' They had saved their money and bought me the most beautiful negligee I ever had in my married life. I had some of the

Marine boys there, the Protestant chaplain stood by me, and the Catholic chaplain married me. So I had a very beautiful military wedding. When we went down to my wedding dinner, a gentleman came over and said how wonderful you and your husband are, you are so happy. He said, 'I am the head of the Library of Congress, and it is my pleasure to buy you all a drink.' He was so nice to us.

Interesting People

I have met many interesting people. I also used to babysit to make money. I made sixty-two dollars and fifty cents a month, which wasn't much. And when you had to buy stockings, lipstick, and various things I babysat for extra money. One of the gentlemen I babysat for was Colonel Beirne Lay, Jr. He wrote *Twelve O'clock High*. He said 'I have a manuscript here all typed, call me if you want to read it. When you get through it, tell me what you think. I hope someday, I can get something for it. Maybe publish it or have a movie made.' He did have a movie made of it! I took care of his baby, and he was a wonderful man. I also took care of a little child for the Biddle family. They were very, very well-known and he was in the Embassy. I met so many people, it was wonderful. I had the pleasure of being in the parade for Admiral Nimitz. Of course, I was one of hundreds of women, but I was in the parade.

Discharged

[I was in the service] from April 6, 1944, through October of 1945. My husband was discharged before me. He was in the Army, in the Signal Corps and discharged in September. I was going to go to Hawaii, but I was married. It was embarrassing for him to be home while his wife was still serving. So I came home. It was the most wonderful time of my life, I thought. I really enjoyed all of it.

The WAVES have their national group. I brought my cap to show you, we wear caps. I thought you should also see the current WAVES paper we have. We keep up with things. The girl that stood up for me at my wedding has come every year to see us. She liked [Saratoga Race Course] horse racing, laugh if you will. I liked it, but I would be working so I would let her go with my husband. Then we got together when I retired. She called about two weeks ago, we keep up. I write to other girls, and we meet up at these conventions that the WAVES nationally have. I am a very fortunate woman.

After the war I was very busy, and I'm still busy being involved with things. I was always happy with people, and through the years I have done a lot of lecturing for women's places in unions. I decided to go back to the telephone company and worked there until my children came along. Then I did not work for sixteen years. Afterward, I went back to the telephone company again, but everything was different. They were going into computers. Then I was asked to be a union representative. I said, 'Well I don't know,' and they said, 'Oh, you are going to do it.' I only lasted a few months being a representative and then went on the executive board of the union. I then felt I might as well go back to school and went to Russell Sage College and Cornell University, for a two-year program for labor management. I came out with all A's and B's, and A's in economics, which was good at the time. I was one of two women in a class of twenty-six down in Albany in the Russell Sage/Cornell group. The men at that time in the 1970s were very insulting. They felt a woman's place was in the home. I remember a couple of them saying, 'Why don't you stay home with your children?'

I said, 'No, I am going to work, and I am going to learn!'

Before I was through, all of the men all stood behind me and said, 'You did fine,' and were really nice to me. I felt that once they knew me, it was great. I loved the union work. After that I did a lot of lobbying in Washington, D.C.

When Hugh Carey ran for Governor of New York, I was non-political as far as saying who I would vote for. But Mary Anne Krupsak, his lieutenant governor, asked me if I would help them. I said I would speak on women's rights and getting out to vote. My children used to say, 'Mom's going to be on TV again.' And I was many times… but I had a strong belief in my country. I believe if people have a mouth, they should open it and speak their opinion. They should not say what anyone should do and then expect to have things done for you, when you don't take an interest in it. So I would go to town meetings and various things, but that is the way I am.

It came easy for me to be in the service. I would write letters and correspond, so I just loved every day of my military career. There were so many things that I was fortunate enough to be involved in and enjoyed meeting people.

Margaret Doris Alund Lear passed away on November 19, 2005, at the age of 82.

CHAPTER FOURTEEN

The Recruiter

Helen Marcil went into the service from a working-class family, following her brothers when the Coast Guard opened up their Women's Reserve, the SPARS. She served as a recruiter, traveling the country. She gave this interview in 2012, at the age of 82.

Helen Marcil Brennan

I was born in Cohoes, New York, on August 21, 1920. I went to Saint Bernard's Grammar School. For high school I went to Catholic High in Troy.

[I remember where I was when I heard about the attack on Pearl Harbor], very vividly I remember. It was on a Sunday, December 7, and we were getting ready for dinner, and we heard it on the radio. My mother started to cry very softly, and I thought, 'Why is she crying?' But she was thinking that she had two sons and she figured they'll be going into the service. My brother and my boyfriend immediately went down the next day and volunteered to enter the service.

My boyfriend, who later became my husband, joined the Navy, and my brother joined the Coast Guard. Years later, I visited the *Arizona* in Pearl Harbor, Hawaii, and what a feeling to know that all those bodies were down there. It was a wonderful experience to go there.

One day I was on my lunch hour from the FBI and there was a recruiting trailer on North Pearl Street [in Albany] and I went over. It was for the SPARS, and so I got all the information. I decided to go into the Coast Guard, the SPARS, because my brother was in the Coast Guard. When I went home, I was all enthused about going into the service. Now, at that point, I was in the FBI, I can just say that I was in correspondence. I ran the switchboard, and I did teletype and all sorts of communications, but we couldn't talk about it. I had a hard time getting a release to go into the service because they said I was doing my duty there, in the FBI. I said I really wanted to go, and I still have a letter from J. Edgar Hoover giving me permission to resign and saying he hoped I'd have a good time in the service.

Well, my father was very old-fashioned, and he had an idea that all servicewomen were 'fast,' as he used to say. He didn't want me to go in, but he didn't stop me. After I was in, he was very proud of me and my sister and my two brothers. He was in World War I, in the Army.

Away From Home

I was sworn in in Albany in August of 1942; I had to meet a group of people in New York City, and I had two suitcases and I thought, 'I'll never make it.' I went all by myself, and I was just about dying, holding my two suitcases. It was my first time away from home and it was my first time going to New York City alone. I was very sheltered, so to speak.

I missed the people at Grand Central Station, and we had to wait and we had a military train, and it took us forever to get to Palm Beach. It was two days for us to get down there, and when we got there to the SPAR station, they billeted us in the Biltmore Hotel, a very swanky hotel that had been taken over by the government. We got in line to get in there and we were starving, and we went right to the mess hall, and when we got to go into the mess hall, the girls that were dishing out the tomatoes and stuff, they all started to say, [*sings in singsong fashion*] 'You'll be sorry!' [*Laughs*]

But it was wonderful, really. The Biltmore Hotel in Palm Beach, we went to classes from nine o'clock in the morning until ten o'clock at night, but it wasn't all classes. During that time we would have drills, we would march, we would have swim and surf, so it was broken up with the classroom studies. It was really wonderful training, and I graduated first in my class from yeoman school.

My sister went in a year after I did; she had to wait to be old enough to go in. I was way ahead of her in yeoman school. Later, it was a good advertisement for the SPARS that two sisters were there. They took advantage of that and let us both be at the same station, to be stationed together, but I was in travel status, and I went all over and did the speeches and all that. My sister was in yeoman work, she did clerical work in the office, she didn't do the traveling I did.

I could have gone to New Orleans or St. Louis, the headquarters. I picked St. Louis, and from St. Louis, because I was a recruiter and I was a good speaker, I used to speak at all of the Rotary Clubs at the towns I went to.

'I Feel Responsible He's Dead'

I had two speeches. I'd look at the crowd and if it looked low key and I thought it should be higher, I would talk more about the casualties of war. But not always. I had a problem that bothered me for years after I got out of the service. When I was up in North Dakota, I was recruiting 18-year-old boys and a young man came in and I interviewed him. He was so thrilled to go into the service! He did the exam and all that, and then he went down to Omaha to be sworn in; it was all through me that he came in. He asked me to come to Sunday dinner with his family, and after always eating in restaurants and hotels, I was thrilled. So on Sunday afternoon, I met his mother and his father, and they told me how thrilled he was that he was going into the service, that he was on cloud nine.

About six months later, he was shipped out and he was on a ship that was torpedoed, and he was killed. I felt responsible for that, I really did. I thought that if I hadn't recruited him, maybe he wouldn't have gone in the Coast Guard. It troubled me a lot. So the next time that I had to go up there to recruit in North Dakota, I thought, 'I can't visit his parents, they'd probably kick me right off their porch.' But I thought, 'I have to do it,' so I called them up and told them I was in town to recruit again, and they invited me to dinner. I went over and I told them how sorry I was.

They gave me a big picture of him.

I said, 'I can't get him out of my mind, I feel responsible that he's dead.'

They said, 'Don't feel like that. It was the most wonderful thing that happened to him. He was so happy.'

So instead of them saying to me, 'You recruited our son and he's dead,' they had open arms for me. I had such a feeling of gratitude that they did that. But that's the only bad memory I have of the service.

Small Towns

A lot of times, I had to go by myself. When it was very small towns in North and South Dakota, I would go by myself and on the train. I remember one small town that I went to, and I wondered why they had sent me there. When I got off the train, I had my suitcase and all sorts of pamphlets and posters, and I asked where I could get a taxi. The man said to me, 'We don't have any taxis, where are you going?'

I told him the hotel and he told me it was about three blocks down, he told me how to get there. So I walked there, and it was like something out of Norman Rockwell. There were four men sitting around a pot-belly stove and when I came in the door, they all turned around and looked at me.

One man stood up and said, 'You must be the recruiter that's coming,' because the Coast Guard had sent my reservations in. They didn't have to because I was the only one in the hotel. [Laughs] He brought me up to the second floor, there was no elevator, and I asked him for my key. He said they didn't normally use keys. I said I had to have a key and he gave me a skeleton key, that's the type of place [it was]. I spent a whole week there by myself. I recruited out of the post office but then when I'd get out of there and go look for a place, there were no restaurants. I went to a bakery and bought food there and went and bought milk. I called up my recruiting office in Omaha and asked if I had to stay a whole week. I didn't interview anyone, and I didn't have any speeches because there was no Rotary or anything like that. [Laughs]

The Band Circuit

Another thing, out of St. Louis, they had all the men that were in all the bands, Glenn Miller and all that, they had a group that went all around the country, like they do now. When they came into Omaha, they came into our office and said they were going to be in the area and going to North and South Dakota and they wanted to take a recruiter with them. They figured the band was there, they'd put on this wonderful concert in the town and the recruiter would be there, maybe getting some people into the service. So they picked me and said that I would go, so I went. I rode in the bus with all of the musicians, and I remember, I was never so cold in my life. We were in Fargo, ND, and it was so cold, unbelievably cold. We put on a concert and as we were coming out of the stage door, there were a lot of grammar school kids there with their autograph books and one little girl came over to me and said, 'Are you anybody?' [*Laughs*]

I told her, 'No, I'm really not.'

I enjoyed that. I traveled with them through Iowa and North and South Dakota while they did their concerts and I sat on the stage. I do not have any musical talent but the man that was in charge of them said they had one number and they were going to use maracas.

He said, 'Helen, when I do this [*motions with hand*], I want you to [shake] the maracas.'

I said, 'Really, I don't have any rhythm, I'm not going to be able to do it.'

'You'll do it.' So I said okay.

When it came time, he went like that [*makes hand motion*] and I threw the whole band off. I did it all wrong and I was so embarrassed.

I said to him, 'I told you I couldn't do it,' and he never asked me to do it again.

He said, 'Stick to your speeches!'

I said, 'I told you I'm not musically inclined!'

Family

When we closed our recruiting station in Omaha, we had our choice of three places to go: Alaska, Hawaii, or Washington. I picked Washington because in the meantime, my husband had come home, and we were married in Omaha. He was a radioman in the Navy. He was on a sub chaser, the same sub chaser for four years. He was in the South Pacific the whole war, but he was going to be discharged from Guam. I wanted to go to Hawaii but I thought I'd better go to Washington, he'll come home in the meantime. He was out on Guam when I was discharged so I really could have gone to Hawaii, but I wouldn't do that, thinking maybe I'd miss him.

Brother Jack

One other very nice thing happened to my sister and me. I was in Omaha at the recruiting office and a military policeman came in.

He said, 'Where are the Marcil sisters?'

We both looked up and said, 'Here we are.'

He said, 'Your brother, Jack, is on a troop train here in Omaha and we have a delay. He said that his sisters were here, and we want to bring you down to see your brother.'

So they brought us down and there was this troop train, all military, and they walked us down and they let my brother get off the train, but we had to stay right there. But we hadn't seen my brother in almost three years so when he said how that happened, he had been in Germany, and he was just ready to come home, and they needed an electrician first class, and they sent him out to the west coast so that he would go to the South Pacific. He was on an LST (Landing Ship, Tank). He mentioned that his sisters were stationed in Omaha so the officer in charge told him that they were going to be in Omaha for a couple of hours and that he would go and get his sisters. I thought that was so nice that they brought us down and that we got to see Jack. We hadn't seen him in three years. We had to stay right there down by the tracks.

My brother, Jack, the one that I'm talking about, he and I are the only two that are still living. My sister's dead and my brother that was in the Navy, the youngest one, he was a pharmacist mate attached to the Marine Corps, he's dead.

One morning I was called, it was the middle of the night, they said, 'Your husband's calling from Seattle, WA.' I spoke to him and I cried through most of the phone call and he said, 'Helen please, let me talk to you. Stop crying!' [Laughs]

He came to Washington. He was discharged from Seattle, Washington, and if your husband was discharged, you automatically could be discharged. All I had to do was produce his discharge and I was discharged, too.

The End of the War

I was in Omaha when [I heard about the death of President Roosevelt], and I was going up the stairs into the USO and two women who were Army recruiters—you knew most of the recruiters of the other services because we would attend different meetings together—were coming down and they told me. That's where I was, in the middle of the flight of stairs on the way to the USO, when I heard he was dead. Another thing that was very emotional for me was seeing General Wainwright; he was in [the Bataan Death March].[25] He came to Washington, and they had a special parade in his honor.

---

[25] *General Wainwright*-Jonathan Wainwright IV (1883-1953) was the Commander of Allied forces in the Philippines at the time Japan surrendered to

General of the Army Douglas MacArthur and Lt. Gen. Jonathan Wainwright greet each other in Yokohama, Japan on August 31, 1945. U.S. Department of Defense, public domain

He was in an open car, and we had to line the streets, all of the different military, and as his car passed where you were standing, you would salute him. He looked like he was coming back from the grave, he was so thin, but I always remember that. That was a highlight in my life, too, that I was there when he was in Washington.

I never regretted my service. I was very patriotic; my whole family was patriotic. My mother and father were so proud of the four stars in the window. The people next door to us had three children in the service and they had three stars. When my young-

the United States. In May 1942, with food and firepower running out, he made the difficult decision to surrender the remaining Allied forces on the Philippines. He became the highest-ranking American prisoner of war, and with his men, suffered the rest of the war maltreated in Japanese prison camps.

est brother, Ned, the one that was in the Navy, went in and we got the fourth star, my father and mother were thrilled.

*

How did the war change my life? It broadened me, meeting so many different types of people from different parts of the country. I never had any negative other than when that young man was killed. It just enriched my life, going into the service. If I hadn't gone into the service, I would have been living in Troy, working at the FBI in Albany, and that would have been it. But I got to go all over the Middle West, and I enjoyed all the people I met. I treasure the years that I was in the service.

CHAPTER FIFTEEN

The WREN

Born near London, England, Kathleen Davie joined the Women's Royal Naval Service at age 17 during the war.[26] Afterwards, she felt a calling to serve God and started training to become a nurse at St. Bartholomew's Hospital in London. Later, she met a Congregational minister who asked her to go to Michigan with his family to care for his three-year-old twins while he did an exchange pastorate for three months. She quit her job and moved to the United States. She married Ralph, a Baptist minister, in February 1966 and moved to New Rochelle, New York, in 1967. She sat

[26] *Women's Royal Naval Service* – "The WRNS was reformed as an auxiliary service for women in April of 1939. It started with 3,400 volunteers working as storekeepers, engineers, draftswomen, radar operators, and weather forecasters. Some also worked as paymasters, secretaries, coders, decoders, writers, depth charge fitters, boiler cleaners, life-belt washers, torpedo net repairers, and hostesses of hostels. WRNS plotters helped with the secret planning for the D-Day invasion. Many Wrens served abroad during the war, in the Middle East and the Far East. By the end of the war, there were 72,000 Wrens." Source: Shuler, Megan, Hudson Falls High School World War II Living History Project, 2006, as researched from Guddant, Soujanya, *In Air and Sea (WAAF and WRNS)*, The Living Archive; *The Women's Royal Naval Service (W.R.N.S.) - A Celebration of Their Lives Then and Now*; Simkin, John, *Auxiliary Territorial Service*. Spartacus Educational; Harris, Carol, *Women Under Fire in World War Two*. BBC.

for this interview with one of my World War II Oral History Project students in 2006 at the age of 79.

Kathleen Mary Davie

I was born on January 28, 1927, in Chiswick, London, England. We were living in a place called Wembley, which is where the soccer cup finals are held, and one of the things that we did when the war broke out was to stand on the landing, halfway up our stairs, and look out over London. At the time that they were announcing the war had started, on September 3, 1939, there was an air raid siren that immediately went off, and of course we were a little scared, and we looked out over London to see if we could see any action, but we couldn't, and it finished shortly after that.[27]

Doodle Bugs

Later, there were bombs around us and we used to hear them. The thing that was the most frightening really was not so much the bombs, because you usually would hear a plane come before you'd hear the bombs, but when they started these unmanned planes called 'doodle bugs.' You'd just hear the engine suddenly start, shut off, and then you'd wait for the crash because there'd be a bomb at the end of that. So, that was a bit unnerving.

---

[27] "The news that Britain was at war was broken by Prime Minister Neville Chamberlain at 11.15am on Sunday 3 September 1939. In a 5-minute broadcast on the Home Service, he announced that as Hitler had failed to respond to British demands to leave Poland, "This country is at war with Germany". Source: 'Chamberlain announces Britain is at war with Germany,3 September 1939.' British Broadcasting Company, www.bbc.com/historyofthebbc/anniversaries/september/war-announced

My father's cousin went into the Women's Naval Service, and I think she went in after I did. I was in the Women's Naval Service. The war broke out when I had just finished the first year of high school, it was county school, and my father decided we had to have an air raid shelter. So, my doll carriage, which was quite a sizeable one—you could have put a small baby in it—became a wheelbarrow for carting rocks and so on for making the air raid shelter, which we did at the bottom of the garden. Most of my high school was during the war. So, we used to sleep in the air raid shelter on a plank about 10 inches wide—amazing, we slept pretty well. And most of our schooling was done either between the classroom or the air raid shelter. We used to take sandwiches to school with us so that if the air raid warnings stayed on too long, we would still have things to eat.

We always had all kinds of snacks. And we had most of our classes in the air raid shelter, a good deal of the time; it just went off at different times, and we would all go to the shelters. We were so used to the routine by the time I got to leaving school, it was just one of the things we did. It was most of my high school.

I left school in '43, so my service was in the fall of '44, after I had spent a year doing secretarial training. My mother thought I would be exempt from military service if I did that, so I volunteered for the WRENs. I don't know that we really thought anything about it until we went to a cousin of my mother's in East Anglia, where part of his farm was annexed to make the aerodrome which was taken over by the American soldiers and fliers. So, I think my mother was a little anti-American, but I married an American, so she had to get over that.

Life in England

I was only in my teens, and I wasn't very politically astute. I don't think that many of my school friends were particularly up on what was happening in politics and national life—we were more concerned with what Germany was doing. Of course, we didn't have television, we had radio, and I remember different things being told to us, that the Germans had bombed this town or that town, and what we had done in retaliation, but of course there were no pictures or anything, like now we have instant pictures of everything. I don't remember being told how many lives were being lost or anything like that. There was also a program that described how the British were putting misleading notices out by radio to Germany, so that they didn't know what damage they had done where. We had code names; I don't remember what they were, but there were code names for different places. I remember we learned a lot more about what had happened, what had been bombed, months afterward.

We had ration books, and a number of coupons had to last for each month and so on, but we didn't have our tea, for instance, we didn't have our tea very strong. We were rationed for meat and eggs, and milk, and sugar and tea, and coffee, mostly the basics. Flour was rationed. My father gave up sugar, and we were always having some things left over that we could hand on to other people who found it more difficult. To this day I only use about one bag of sugar a year, simply because we got used to doing that. And we had coupons for everything, and it lasted for quite a while. We used to eat and sleep, and we used to play games, like board games. 'Old Draughts' we used to play, which is the same as your checkers. We'd do that, but we read a lot, my sister and I were both readers, and we'd sit and read, talk.

We had an incendiary bomb land on our house, but the air raid warden saw it very quickly and put the fire out. We never even lost the house; we lost the front gate; the incendiary bomb destroyed the gate in the front yard. We were very blessed. The Jerries were really smart; they used to have a high-explosive bomb that started things off, and then they put an incendiary bomb just as everybody was trying to rescue people. Our shelter was in the backyard, way at the farthest end of the backyard. My father had built a rockery, a rock garden, with a channel down the middle of it, and the shelter was right behind it, so it sort of looked like it was part of the rock garden.

The Girl Guides

My father was in the Signal Engineer Office for London Transport, and was seventy feet below ground in an office for London Transport. If there was a bomb on the land destroying some tunnels or train tracks or anything like that, he would be the one that would have to stop and repair and make sure that the trains didn't go into the danger area. So, he had an interesting time, but it was mostly nighttime work for him. He used to write to me when I was in Ireland, and the letters used to come like a paper doily with chunks taken out of it, because of the way they used to censor everything. It was just from Britain over to Ireland, and I used to think it was crazy that they censored so much, but they did it so that the enemy would not find out what was happening. Nowadays, I don't know how they do the censoring at all because of the e-mails and everything else. It's just a mind-boggling task.

One of the things that I volunteered to do was to go and do dishwashing at the hospital. We didn't have dishwashers in those days, we didn't even have refrigerators. I was in the... well, you call it Girl Scouts, Girl Guides they call it.

We used to go and work at the hospital and do all sorts of volunteer work during the war. Bicycles were very much used. You either walked or we rode places. I mean we lived in London, but we used to bike ride a lot when we were kids. Nowadays it seems strange that kids can't go out. We went miles, we were gone for a whole day and our parents never even thought anything of it. Now, you're sort of checking in with your parents all the time if you go out. Kids—we were very free and the war changed a lot of that. I'm sure it did here too. Our private lives are more restricted nowadays.

There were times when we felt threatened, and there were times when we were pleased. Everybody was rejoicing at the news of the D-Day landings. Of course, the thing that had been badly fought at was the Dunkirk debacle. A lot of my friends were evacuated to country places, so that was another difficult thing for a lot of people, to have their kids go away. Some even sent them to the States. Every so often I meet someone who came over as an evacuee. They married an American and stayed.

I think the morale was exceptionally good. I really do. I can't remember any specific ways in which people did it, but of course Winston Churchill was the prime minister that really boosted people's morale, I think. We were so busy, involved in the war effort in different ways. People were air raid wardens, and people were volunteering—everybody volunteered in some way to do something that would help the war effort. The threat of Germany invading Britain, I think, increased the amount of activity that people were involved with. We were at war now, but we're not at war on our own land, whereas the bombs were falling all the time.

The WRENs

In the WRENs, I did mostly the typing of signals. Many of them had been decoded by the coding group, and then we would type them and send them to the admiral and various other people. It was quite an interesting job. We did shift work—working all night and then having the day off, and then working the following evening, and then the next morning and so on, and then it would be the same over again. So, we never knew, we had to get used to sleeping at all odd hours.

I enjoyed being in the WRENs, in Northern Ireland; the Irish Sea separated England from Northern Ireland, and when I was first sent there, it was very, very rough. We were hanging on for dear life in order to stay on the boat, and it was a small boat; people talk about the Irish Sea being rough all the time. We weren't allowed to go over the border into southern Ireland because they were not involved in the war, and if we did, we were told we had to take off our uniforms and wear [civilian dress]. In Belfast, the problems that the Catholics and the Protestants had, even then, was quite strong. I remember I was very friendly with a Catholic girl who was my bunkmate, and I took her to the Baptist church with me, and the preacher inveighed against the Catholics in such a way that I said I would never go back to that church. So, although I'm now a Baptist minister, I would never have gone back to that church. And I went to her church with her most of the rest of the time I was in Belfast.

Religious wars were still going on during the war; it's never really been settled, even though there's peace there now. That was very strange in Belfast because the Catholic population in Belfast were against the war and were against the British—they have always been against the British, I guess. So, we were told never to go down certain streets, which was largely a Catholic area in Belfast, in our uniform. But I loved Ireland; it was a beautiful place. If we were in the Castle, which was up on a hill, we used to be able, early in the morning if we'd been there all night, we'd look out toward the sun rising over the hills of Scotland across the Irish Sea, and we were able to see from there. Princess Elizabeth came over when she was, I think, eighteen, which was evidently a year after I had been in Belfast for that time. She came over and launched an aircraft carrier, and I don't remember the name of it, but I was down at the docks and watched her throw the bottle at the hull.

[The Castle] was where we did a lot of decoding of messages. Things were sent from ships in the Irish Sea, and around Britain and Northern Europe. Messages were sent and decoded, so that we knew what the Germans were doing. It was all very hush-hush, but when the things were decoded, they had to go to the various people who could take any action, if there was action needed. It was very interesting. Of course, now it's all done with computers. We had teleprinters, which were ways of sending messages that would be like the forerunner of the computer, I think. Sending messages from England to Northern Ireland, or from ships at sea, would come by teleprinter and telephone messages, too.

I didn't hear about [the atomic bombs and the fallout] until quite a long while afterwards. I was horrified that we would use a nuclear bomb. I think that was something that we never should have done, but we did it. There's a lot of things we regret about the war. There's a lot of things that are still only now coming to light about that war. I saw a program on television just recently that showed some places that nobody knew anything about at the time. I think there were ways in which the lack of communication, such as we know communication nowadays, was probably useful to the war effort, because the enemy couldn't find out an awful lot. Whereas now, I cringe sometimes when I see things on television that I think could help Al Qaeda or the insurgents in Iraq. I just wonder sometimes whether a lot of the things that we talk about, our security things and everything, whether we're being wise in publicizing as much as we do. But that's probably because I was so lacking in information during the war.

War's End

I was in Belfast at the time the war ended, on duty in the Castle of Belfast, which had been taken over by the Navy, and we decided we had to celebrate somehow, so a group of us walked down the hill to the bottom where there was an ice cream shack, and we brought back ice creams to everybody to celebrate. And then there was a big celebration in London. I think it wasn't until the next year, if I remember rightly, and there was a big celebration in London and we went. Some friends of mine that now live in Canada and I went into the city. We were young enough to not mind the crowds then, but it was a fun time. Everybody was just waving flags and just having a good time. It was a bit like Times Square at New Year's. It was very busy. I don't know how we got there— probably by subway.

*

I think, in general, most of us felt bad that civilians were being killed. Factories that were turning out good things for people were also being bombed because we had ideas that they were producing munitions. I think a lot of things happened where we think something is true, and then after we bombed it, we discover—like we did with weapons of mass destruction in Iraq—that it wasn't true. I don't really know anything about covert operations during the war, but I'm sure there were. We had a young man come from

France who was British—he'd grown up in France—and his father was killed and he went underground with the French Maquis to fight against the Germans in a sort of underground way. He came and lived in Britain, lived next door to us for quite a while. He and his friends were all sort of underground. The Germans didn't even know about what was going on, and what they were doing, sabotaging a lot of German things.

I went into nursing after the war. The war was over in '45, in May, and then in August, and in '46, in September, I started nursing training, because I felt called to do missionary work. I applied to the hospital and was accepted and did four years at St. Bartholomew's Hospital in London. Part of that time we were still evacuated. Some of the wards had been evacuated during the war and they hadn't moved back to London because there wasn't really any room.

It seemed to me that even after I was doing nursing training, after the war, in some ways things were not greatly changed even though the war was over. We were still rationed for a while.

'Life Has Changed'

I didn't move to the United States until 1960. That was partly because I had gone to India as a missionary, and was there for two years, and I went to India expecting the culture to be very different and the language to be different. When I came to the States in 1960, which was seven years after I had gone to India, I expected the language to be the same, and it isn't by a long way. It's even worse now, I don't understand half the language that you guys talk about. [Laughs] And I really suffered a great deal more culture shock coming here than I did going to India, because I was prepared for it there. I had to learn to talk American, and now it's gotten to the point where I can't tell the difference—I don't know whether an expression is a British expression or whether it's an American expression.

So, life has changed a great deal in fifty years; I think the world has changed a great deal. We didn't have television until 1952. My father built his own television set. I watched Wimbledon. That was the first thing I saw. I had just had an appendectomy, and I lay on the couch and watched tennis and Wimbledon on this new TV that my father had built. That made a big difference to our lives. I still prefer the radio. I like to use my imagination when I hear stories and so on, instead of having it all presented to me in picture form.

Anti-War

Student interviewer: How do you feel about bombing against civilians in Germany by the British and Americans?

I just thought it was terrible that we were bombing, and they were bombing us. But what can you do? I've never felt that we should ever retaliate against somebody, because usually what happens in war is you bomb each other to death, and then negotiate afterwards. Well, we could negotiate beforehand. I think we very often want to show our power or something and we are not so willing to go the whole mile with negotiation. I'm very anti-war. Mostly I think because I was in it. I don't know whether if I were seventeen and a half now, whether I would volunteer to go to Iraq. I rather think I would not because I just don't feel that war is the answer. Maybe if I was younger, I'd be... I'm more politically astute now than I was when I was seventeen. There's a lot of difficult questions that we all have to think about.

Kathleen M. Davie passed away on January 1, 2020 at the age of 92.

PART FOUR

WAR BRIDES

"My sister had a falling out with the local vicar because he was against our marriage and saying [bad] things about the American soldiers. My sister was in the church youth group and stood up for me, saying, 'That is my sister, and she is married to an American. I wish you would not talk that way.' And she never went back to the youth center. There were reservations about it. Some had horror stories, other brides. I was lucky. Yes, we were warned about how there were mixed feelings about it."

—War bride, Great Britain

CHAPTER SIXTEEN

The War Brides

Joyce Griffin was raised in England on the family farm with her sister. During the war years she served in the British Women's Army as a physical education instructor and then as a secretary and married US Army Sgt. John J. Griffin, who was serving there at the time. John was injured and returned to the United States for medical treatment; Joyce followed aboard a Red Cross ship with many other war brides several months later. This interview was given at our high school in 2004, when she was eighty-two years old.

Joyce Griffin

I was born October 6, 1922, in Helsby, in the county of Cheshire, England. My father was a British naval officer in World War I. It was very strict during the war. For example, you would have only two ounces of butter, two ounces of margarine, and four ounces of cheese. Everything was rationed like that. It was very difficult. I was lucky because I was raised on a poultry farm. We had all those supplies—even though I did not like any of those products and still don't! At least we could exchange them on the black market.

I eventually came to join the British Army Auxiliary Territorial Service. My parents did not object to it. I had wanted to go into what was called the Women's Land Army where you were assigned to farms and so forth. I had an interest in nature. But my father did not think that was appropriate for a young lady. You had to be checked out by your own doctor rather than a military doctor. So my father beat me to my doctor, they had a discussion, and I was turned down. [Laughs] So then I was conscripted into the women's services; at that time it was just the Army that had opened. At age nineteen you were conscripted.[28]

The ATS

In the ATS, we took shorthand and did typing.[29] Originally, I was the secretary to a naval commander. He was getting rather old

---

[28] *Women's Land Army*-"Though not strictly a military auxiliary force, the Women's Land Army greatly aided the war effort. About 80,000 women joined this group, which had also been in existence during the First World War, in order to grow enough food to support their country. The volunteers learned basic skills that they needed at places such as Agricultural Colleges and then went to live in hostels with other WLAs. They worked several farms, traveling between them during the day and returning to their lodgings at night, sometimes as late as 9:30 PM. They had to take over any work that had been left by men who went to war. Sometimes, they worked alongside Italian and German prisoners of war. They were paid very low wages by the government but were sometimes hired by a specific farmer." Source: Shuler, Megan, Hudson Falls High School World War II Living History Project, 2006, as researched from Kemp, Pat. *First-Hand Account of life in the WLA.* The Wartime Memories Project.

[29] *ATS*-"During the 1930s, when it seemed obvious that a war would start, Britain decided to resurrect her World War I era auxiliary services. In Sep-

and being phased out. His replacement was chosen, and I had to replace a civilian testing the rockets, so I wound up being with a battery of men who were a unit who were experimenting with rockets. It was a highly secret place because rockets were unknown in those days. We would freeze some of the rockets to see how they would fire at low temperatures. And then heat some to see how they would fire in hot countries. We would fire them over the Cardigan Bay, part of the Irish Channel. I was also the physical education instructor. There were different phases. I don't know, there was a unit of ATS girls, but everyone was secret from the others. Soldiers were in each place. It was in South Wales and quite fun. I used to be able to go up onto the lookout area on the roof of the building with the captain of the unit. We would have stopwatches and time the explosion of the rockets in the air and as they splashed into the sea. Then I would have to compile the two results. Sometimes we had visiting officers from other countries. I was there for three years; we could not talk about it. But some of my most memorable experiences were, number one, I met my husband. He was with an American company stationed not too

---

tember 1938, the Auxiliary Territorial Service was formed; women aged 17 to 43 worked as clerks, cooks, and storekeepers. They received two-thirds the pay of male soldiers and were volunteers. In 1939, 300 ATS women were with the British Expeditionary Force in France working on anti-aircraft crews. They were not officially allowed to fire the guns but worked on searchlight crews instead. Some of these women who had been serving as telephone operators were with the last people to be evacuated from Dunkirk on May 26, 1940. In July 1941, the ATS finally earned military status; by September of the same year, it boasted 65,000 women serving as orderlies, postal workers, drivers, and ammunition inspectors in addition to their previous employment. By 1945, 190,000 women worked in increasingly demanding jobs, such as radar operators, military police, and gun crews." Source: Shuler, Megan, Hudson Falls High School World War II Living History Project, 2006, as researched from Simkin, John, *Auxiliary Territorial Service*. Spartacus Educational, and Harris, Carol, *Women Under Fire in World War Two*. BBC.

many miles from where we were. They were sort of experimenting with the same ideas about rockets and tanks.

Bombings

When the bombing of London occurred, I was mostly in South Wales. The bombing had started before I was in the Army; my mother, my sister, and I used to sleep under the stairs every night. We could hear the hum of the German planes coming. They had a very distinctive sound. I don't know how my poor mother ever slept since there was not very much room with the three of us there. My father worked nights then. But we survived. We did not have too many bombs around us, [but the ones that fell] did kill some cows and made a few craters in the ground. It was scary, though, because you would get the impression your name could be on that bomb coming down. I was in Liverpool during a bad bombing raid. We were two stories underground. We were fine, but when we came out in the morning the stores had been bombed, the goods were all over the street, and you heard people calling out that had been buried under the rubble. It was a horrible experience.

[The bombing of Pearl Harbor in Hawaii was not a big deal to the British people], I don't really think so. Just like the bombing of London did not mean much to the American people because it was so far away. Pearl Harbor was the same story. We were still going through the war ourselves in England. We talked of invasions and so forth while we were battling over there; we had landed on the beaches. That is what we were more interested in at the time, I guess.

It was alarming because we did not know if we were going to be overrun at any time. The bombs kept falling. We had the ack-ack [anti-aircraft] guns going off all the time, shooting at the

German planes. We witnessed a few [Royal Air Force] Spitfire fights in the sky. Those were marvelous machines. I can't say it was a good feeling, we were at war, and it was kind of scary at times.

'A Life's Souvenir'

The Americans did not come until 1942, I think. I met John in 1943. It's a funny story about how I met him. His unit was putting on a little show for the local people and I was invited. I didn't really get to know him at that time but his part in it was up on the stage with a top hat and cane. He sang 'Who Threw the Overalls in Mrs. Murphy's Chowder?' [Laughs] Then I met him through some friends. There was a service person's canteen there in the town of Cardigan. We started going out and then became engaged before he went back to Europe. He came over on marriage leave some months later, sometime in February. Of course, he could not get into the establishment; when I got up there, I was shocked to see him. He was here on marriage leave and I was not a bit prepared! My poor mother had a hard time gathering up stuff. She only had the C-rations, some food and clothing. But she managed to beg and borrow and maybe steal, I don't know. It was enough to have a wedding. Of course, his parents did not approve and neither did mine. They thought we should wait until the end of the war. But you never know what is going to happen in a war. They wrote and sent him packages. When John was leaving the States for Europe his father had told him, 'Don't be bringing home any of those limies!' And of course, he did, he called me his 'life's souvenir'.

My sister had a falling out with the local vicar because he was against our marriage and saying [bad] things about the American soldiers. My sister was in the church youth group and stood up for me, saying, 'That is my sister and she is married to an American. I wish you would not talk that way.' And she never went back to the youth center. There were reservations about it. Some had horror stories, other brides. I was lucky. Yes, we were warned about how there were mixed feelings about it.

John was sent back by an Army hospital because he had developed an allergy while he was in Belgium. They did not know what it was and shipped him to an Army hospital in Paris where he was stationed. It all turned out to be related to a stray dog that John had taken in, because he had asthma. He was assigned to a group that was called French Quislings, collaborators that had Nazi leanings. They put him to work with some of the French Quislings repairing the hospital equipment. That is where he got his X-ray burns. Of course, John did not speak French, they did not speak English, and they worked on an X-ray machine. There were some cross-signals, so he did not know the power was on as he was checking the machine. He leaned on it with his knee and his hand and got X-ray burns. He was in a hospital for over a year. It was pretty bad. They shipped him back to the United States for skin grafting. He was back here when the war ended; John was in a group that released some prisoners from a concentration camp. I don't recall which one. So he was finally shipped back to an Army hospital in the United States for treatment, which lasted a year. He came back in November of 1945. I came here to the States in April 1946.

*

I was on a Red Cross ship full of brides and babies of American soldiers, the *Willard H. Holbrook,* a lot of Red Cross nurses and mothers with babies and infants. It was a very rough crossing. We who were able to keep standing would crawl in and the smell of that nursery in the mornings was awful because so many babies were seasick. John met me in New York on crutches.

[Being a 'war bride'] was scary because of the reports we were getting that the American people were against us. They said we were taking up spaces that their soldiers coming home should have. They were told the soldiers were sleeping on park benches because of us. So it was not too great in New York. I said I wanted to get out of here, I don't like this place. We went back to Connecticut where he was from the next day.

VE Day

I was still in the Army when the end of the war was announced. Still stationed at the same place. I was in the South Wales Regiment. I had a Welsh Dragon as our insignia. I wore crossed swords, which indicated I was a Physical Education instructor. I had kept that patch for some time but can't find it now.

On VE Day, we had a great time. It was such a glorious moment meaning the war was over. There was dancing in the street and overall mayhem. I think Churchill announced it on the radio, I guess we were all called to gather around a radio so we could hear his speech. He was such a great man and really held the country together. It was wonderful just to hear his voice; he kept everyone's spirits up. Just to hear his voice was uplifting. We thought Field Marshal Montgomery was pretty great, too. We didn't know much about him really, but we thought he was a savior in many ways along with Winston. But I remember that several months later, there was still a lot of rationing. We went to a restaurant and one of the main meals was still baked beans or sardines on toast. [Laughs] Times were still hard, however, and the long ration cues remained; I stood in those lines too. You would hear about a store that got a shipment of cigarettes. They were little five-in-a-pack sizes. You stood in line for hours trying to get five cigarettes. And it is such a horrible habit! I'm glad I don't do it anymore.

[How do I feel about the German people today?] Oh gosh, that was then and this is now. I have no bad feelings about the Germans; it wasn't the German people, it was the Nazism that we were against, but it still disturbs me that we did not know [that the Holocaust] was going on. It was a horror.

Joyce Griffin passed away on March 20, 2017 at the age of 94.

One of four children, Joan Hoffman was born in Canada in 1923. At the age of six, her father had saved up enough money to send Joan, her mother, and her three siblings to Cambridge, England to visit relatives for six months, but just when the Hoffman family was preparing to head back to Canada, a cable was sent from their father which stated to stay in England, and that he was going to join them in there, managing a horse riding school where she would grow up and meet the American GIs who came to ride in their off duty hours. She eventually wound up marrying one of them and emigrated to the United States after the war.

Joan Hoffman

I was born in Canada in 1923. My mother and father went to Canada after the First World War, and we were there for about six years, and there were four of us born there. And then my father sent Mommy and we four kids home to England for six months to meet our relatives, because he was one of thirteen children and Mother was one of nine. And we were getting ready to come back to Canada, having visited everybody, when Mother got a cable from Dad saying, 'Stay there, I'm coming home!' And you know in those days, children never asked any questions of parents.

And the only thing we could think of was, Dad never had a decent job in Canada. He worked in a flour mill and a mine. And I think he borrowed the money to send us there but stayed and worked there until he got the money and paid for it and then came back to England. So, we were in England from then on.

The Riding School

We were fortunate because when we first went over there, my father got a job managing a riding school. So, we had horses. Basically, our lives revolved around the horses. The stable yard was in the middle of Cambridge, which was a big university town. We went to school, but you had to walk to school, and it had to be a good mile or two from the house. We walked and we rode bicycles. We never had a car, but we had horses. And kids... I never knew it until after I was talking to some girls that I graduated with. We went to Perse High School for girls. And they used to be talking and saying, 'Let's go for a swim,' because the river Cam went all the way around Cambridge. And they had two or three places which were made into bathing steps so that you could go swimming there. And I used to feel, 'Oh I wish I could go with them.' But I knew I had to go home because my father needed me. We worked in the yard. I mean we had grooms there sometimes. We had the horses' livery there. But I mean, the horses had to be fed every day and the stables mucked out and groomed. So, we were always busy with the horses. But the other girls, I heard, were so jealous. They used to think, 'You can go riding anytime you like.' We used to have to go riding whether we wanted to or not, because you know, it was just one of the things. That was even after I left school and got a job, he still would sometimes call me early in the morning, because we had a field that was two miles from the house. We used to turn out a couple of the horses there if they had been working very hard, let them have a day or two in the field. They could just relax. But when you wanted them again, he'd sometimes call me at 4:30 or 5 in the morning and say, 'I want you to get up and go fetch the two horses.' So, I'd walk the two miles and get the horses and come back and have breakfast and give the horses to him. And I get changed and then go to school.

Leading the Horses

But I have to tell you, it was war time and just up the road from our field, there was a small factory that was making some small article that was necessary for the war. And every morning as I was coming home, I would see these... oh, many, many dozens and dozens of elderly men, older men riding their bicycles to go to the little factory further up. And I just saw them and used to say hello. But one time I was starting to lead the two horses, and I couldn't get on them, and so I was walking them home and one of the men riding his bicycle said, 'Would you like a leg up?' So, I said, 'Oh, thank you.' So, he got off his bicycle and put his bicycle down and put his lunchbox down and gave me a leg up. So, I didn't have to walk home. I saw them every day. They didn't know who I was, and I certainly didn't know who they were, but it was just nice. And you won't believe that fifteen years ago, the last time I went back to England to stay with my sister, I was told she had a group of ladies with her. And I was talking to one of the ladies and she said to me, 'Do you still live in Cambridge?'

I said, 'No. I married a Yank. And I've just come from the States to visit my sister.'

So, I said, 'Do you live in Cambridge?'

She said, 'No, we live on Madingley Road. But you would know that because that's a road that goes outside of Cambridge.'

I said, 'I know Madingley Road because we used to have a field up there. And my father used to send me up there to get horses when he needed them.'

She said, 'Would you believe that when we were living there years ago, we'd be in bed and it would be 5:30, maybe quarter to six, and we'd hear clip clop, clip clop, clip clop.' And she said, 'I couldn't understand what that was, so I'd get up and move the curtain and look outside.'

And she said, 'There'd be a young girl and a young boy riding horses and they would be singing. And they would look and if they saw me, they would wave at me.'

I said, 'Well, that was me and my brother. Because my brother said if we're awake, everybody should be awake. So, we sang loudly.'

But what are the chances of meeting a lady? I mean I've been here sixty-three years, so I've been gone from them for forty-five years to meet someone who actually knew or saw us.

I lived in Cambridge. And Cambridge is in East Anglia, which is a flat part of the country, and there were airfields around and a couple of them were taken by the GIs, taken over by the Americans when they came. There wasn't too much in the way of entertainment around. So, they went and bring the GIs in; well, any of the people, servicemen, would be brought into Cambridge in trucks if they had a forty-eight-hour pass. And the largest hotel there was taken over by the Red Cross. I was four when we went to England. I finished school when I was seventeen, and worked for a couple of years. And then got involved with one of those GIs. To tell you the truth, we as kids or even growing up, we never knew much about what was going on. Of course, everything was rationed, the normal people—I don't mean lords and ladies, those who had plenty of money. But those who had a car had to just leave them or get rid of them because the gas was rationed, and people couldn't afford it. We rode bicycles. When my youngest brother was born, they had seats that you sit behind them and babies that could sit up. Mother did all of the shopping with a basket in front of the bicycle, very different from the living you notice now over here too, you know. But it was good, it was good. And my sister went into the Navy, the WRENs, the women's Navy. My brother, just younger than me, was in the tank corps. And he was stationed in Italy, and he married an Italian girl and took her home. They said our family was like the League of Nations, but it was fun. It was very good.

My mother was a volunteer in the large hotel that was given to the Red Cross, and it was GIs that stayed there. And she was in charge of the breakfast on Sundays. And she worked with a friend of hers, who had a small restaurant.

Air Raids

My father, of course, had the riding school. But during the war, he joined the [Home Guard], they used to have places where people would go and sit, and anytime a plane came over, they would report it to headquarters. And he did that during the night. He would work during the night. When the sirens went off for a bomb attack coming, wherever the planes were coming from, there were several of these places. And the one that he worked with was like in the cellar of the Chamber of Commerce. It was a huge room. And they had a huge table with a map of the whole of England. They had to say, 'Well, there's a bomb coming over and it's going northwest and it's going...' so that they knew where they were, you know. We had a siren going off almost anytime, I would say almost every day. But there weren't many bombs dropped on Cambridge because we were surrounded by airfields.

And of course, anti-aircraft groups around the airfields were taking care of them. And I only know of one person who was killed by a bomber, and it was a teacher who taught second grade. She and her mother lived one block from the school. And there was one night where we had air raids and there were a couple of bombs dropped, and one bomb dropped right on her house and the two of them were killed. I mean, there were one or two others but really no real numbers from Cambridge. Although, as I say, theoretically, when we had an air raid siren, we were meant to go downstairs. A lot of people had air raid shelters done in their yard. They'd dig a little and then put corrugated metal roofs. And they'd have like bunks in there. The government also supplied tables made out of metal that you put underneath your table. If you had a square table and if there was an air raid and you had children and you didn't have anywhere to go outside, you would get under there. Because that would be like steel protection. That's what we did. An air raid shelter, especially in London, of course, they had lots of them down there. But they were underground places. And in London everybody went to the train stations, and they put up bunks in there. And people would sleep in there because you were underground. London was a very busy place. But they say that during the war, I think the trains stopped running. Whole families used to go down there and sit there with the children in the bunk and stay overnight. We knew that they were building those things. There were big air raids in some parts of the towns. As I say, they dug them out. Anybody could go there. If you lived there, you'd go. But we didn't have anyone. Well, Father was working. He wasn't there, and Mother was busy. We just stayed in bed. We really didn't have many bombs dropping in Cambridge.

The GIs in England

There was plenty of room for the GIs to stay. There wasn't too much to do. There were only two movie houses, and one restaurant had a dance every Saturday. And then, of course, they could go on the River Cam and punt. No boats were allowed with motors on, just, you know, a canoe or something like that. So, they used to walk through town and our stable yard was in town. And they'd come to the stable yard. There were horses for hire and my father would greet them, 'Hello, can I help you?'

'We want to take a ride.' And my father had one question he asked. No matter who it was, if it was somebody he didn't know, he would say, 'Have you ever been on a horse before?' Because we had some horses that needed to have a rider on it. And there was one guy that came in, sometimes six or seven or eight, but some member of the family had to take them out because they didn't know how to get out of the town of Cambridge to get out into the countryside. So, we literally met up with hundreds of different GIs. It was a very interesting time in our lives, you know, but it was good.

War Bride

Well, there were two GIs that came to ride one day. My father greeted them and said to them his usual thing. And so, he said, 'Have you ever been on a horse before?' And one of the GIs said, 'Sure, I have.' He said, 'I came from Iowa. I've had horses.' So, my father said, 'Okay, fine. My daughter will take you out.' My sister took them out for a ride. And we used to ride.

There were several different places that had horses for hire, but most people used to rent them out for an hour and pay by the hour. You want a ride, it'll cost you so much an hour. But my father wouldn't do that because what we found out is if anybody paid seven and six to ride for an hour, they'd go as far as they could in that hour, and then so they wouldn't have to pay extra if it took them longer to get back, they'd turn around and race the horses back so that they got back within the hour, depending how much trotting and cantering they did. My sister took those out and the next week they came again, and she took them out again. And a third week they came, and she took them out. They had finished riding and said hello and goodbye and they'd gone back to the field.

My father came to me and said, 'Look, if those two GIs want to ride again, you make an appointment and you take them out. And for heaven's sake, teach that one to ride. He's ridden my horse three times. He still looks like a sack of potatoes tied in the middle, and I won't let him ride my horse again.' He said, 'It's a disgrace to my yard; you take them out and teach him to ride.' So, the next time they wanted to ride, I took them out. The streets in the older part of Cambridge were very narrow. You couldn't have horses. So, in town you rode in twos. When my sister took them out, she rode and had the one guy from Iowa ride with her, and the other guy just rode behind. Well, when I took them out, I had him riding beside me. I didn't know at the time, but he came from Jersey City. He had never seen a mounted horse except when the police patrolled the parks. Apparently, I was very strict with him, and I taught him to ride. They never came to ride again. [*Laughs*] But he started dating me, and I eventually married him. So, he taught me to drive his car when I'd been over here six years. And that was the hardest decision he ever had to make, to teach a woman to drive his most precious possession, his car, even though, apparently, I taught him to ride. [*Laughs*]

We met literally hundreds of [GIs]. They were very nice. One man came and he was a very nice guy. I took him out riding. And I was asking him where he was stationed. Anyhow, when I came in that night, I said, 'I had one of your GIs riding today. And I took him out, and we had a nice ride.' Two days later, he came to me and said, 'I was talking to one of the GIs when we were having dinner,' or something and he said, he told me, 'You know, two days ago, I went into Cambridge, and I went for a ride. And I had a wonderful time. It was a very nice girl that took me. And I'm going back there again.' So, my husband said, 'Was the girl a blonde or a brunette?' He said, 'Oh, the girl was a blonde.' My husband said, 'The blonde is my wife.'

He said, 'Oh! I didn't know that.' He never came back again. There was nothing wrong. There's nothing much you can do when you're both on horses, you know what I mean. We laughed at those things. We met many, many lovely guys. We had a good time.

London

In 1944, I was asked to go to London. The firm that I worked for was Pye Radios that was outside of Cambridge. And before the war they made radios for everything, cars. And they were just beginning to make the TVs, but they hadn't started selling them yet. But then they started making radios for tanks or submarines or airplanes. They were doing all war work. And I worked there for some time. And then they said they had an office in London and they said they really needed someone to go and work in the office because the girls that worked there had evacuated. During the war they evacuated many families from the big towns and sent them to the smaller cities and found houses, families who would take them. Well, we had a house with plenty of room. But when I was asked if I wanted to go, I said yes. So, I went up to London and got accommodations right in the place near where I was going to work. There was a youth hostel for young girls who were going to live in London for the first time. And you could only stay there for two years because they figured if you'd be in London, and had a job and worked for two years, you could find somewhere else to live. But I didn't know how long I was going to be there. So, I got a job there. My bedroom was on the third floor.

Every time there was an air raid warning, you had to go down to their cellar. And then when the all-clear went, you'd go back to bed. Well, sometimes you'd do that three times a night. Because as the waves of bombers came over, another siren would go off. But then another batch would come. I got tired. I said, 'This is ridiculous getting up two or three times a night and having to go back upstairs.' So, they had a small air raid shelter in their yard, and it had six bunks in there. I said to this girl, 'I'm going to sleep down there.' So, instead of going upstairs to our bedrooms, we slept there. We could hear the siren, and we could hear the bombs go. But that was the beginning of what they called the 'buzz bombs'; the first bombs at this time had motors on them. After the air raid siren would go, you'd often here this 'putt, putt, putt.' And you knew that it was a bomb coming over. But all of a sudden, it would stop, and then it fell.

I was only there for six months, because, well, I was going to get married. So, I went home and got married. I wanted to go back to the company I was in, and I told them, I said, 'I might have to leave without very much notice.'

They said, 'Oh well, we don't want you here then.' So, I had no job. My husband was in the Eighth Air Force. He wasn't a flyer, he was a secretary. So he got all of the letters and information that came in first. He came in one day and said, 'We just got a notice today that at the end of the war, the Eighth Air Force is going to be sent to Germany in the Army of Occupation.'

He said, 'If I'm in Germany in the Army of Occupation and I get leave, they won't give me leave to go from Germany to England to see you. They'll give me leave to go from Germany to the States where I'm from.'

So, he said, 'The best thing to do is to get you there now.'

So, we went up to the embassy. I had my paperwork and because I had a Canadian birth certificate, I would be returning to the continent of my birth. And they issued me a non-cultural visa. Now for the thousands of other girls that had to wait until the end of the war, I don't know. But they said, 'Go home and pack your clothes, pack whatever you want to take with you, and be ready to leave in twenty-four hours' notice.'

So, we went there to Cambridge, and I said to my mother, 'I've got to pack everything because I have to be ready to leave in twenty-four hours' notice.'

She said, 'All right then, pack.' So, two days later, I hadn't heard anything. And I said to my mother, 'Would you wash the clothes that I'm wearing, because I have to be ready to leave and I would like to take them with me.'

Well, we didn't have a washing machine or anything. So, Mother washed them by hand, you know. And two or three days later, I said, 'Would you wash these?'

After doing that for two weeks, she said to me, 'Look, I am not going to spend the rest of my life washing your clothes. If you get the notice to go, and you've got dirty clothes, either wear them dirty or pack them dirty or leave them here and I'll take care of them. They didn't send me any notice until six months later! So, it was just as well that she hadn't been washing all that time.

I just sort of went about my business. Because the company that I had worked for in London, 'If you're going to leave without giving us two weeks' notice, no, we don't want you.' So, I worked with my father. When the GIs came to ride, it had been mostly my sister who would take them out. When I was there, I worked with my father. My husband was very fortunate. He used to get a pass to come into Cambridge every night. So, after he'd finish his work in the office, he'd get on his bicycle and start riding the fourteen miles to Cambridge. And I would've been taking GIs or whoever else went riding. So, if I finished the night, I'd get on my bike and go and meet him. And then he'd ride and stay overnight and get up at four or five in the morning, and I'd give him breakfast. And then, I would ride my bicycle with him back, but I wasn't allowed on the base, because I was just a civilian. So, he'd say goodbye to me and he'd go on and he was there. And then I'd turn around and ride the fourteen miles back by myself. But that's what you did.

'She'll Never Leave Me'

We were called by the embassy in London and told on a Saturday. They sent a cable; because I was out riding with four or five GIs, and my youngest brother knew where we went riding, he came on his bicycle, 'Joan, you got a cable! You gotta go! You gotta go!'

That was Saturday afternoon. The cable said: 'Report to the embassy in London at nine o'clock on Monday morning, being prepared to pay your passage and sail.' So, I packed up and everything, and we went up to London. My husband of course couldn't go. They sent me by train from London to Southampton, which is in the south of England, because that's where the boat was. We got on board, but my husband wasn't allowed to come to the boat with me. So, he went back to Cambridge to say to my mother and father, 'I've sent her on her way.'

Now they both liked him, but he said to me afterwards in a letter, 'It was a little chilly about your father.' Because somebody had once said to him, 'Cap, what are you going to do when your daughter leaves you?'

He said, 'What do you mean when my daughter leaves me?'

He said, 'Oh, I'm sorry. I heard she'd married a Yank.'

He said, 'She did marry a Yank.'

And he said, 'Oh, well I presumed that he would be going to the States.'

He said, 'She married a Yank, but she'll never leave me.' So, when the time actually came, see, it was a little bit of a shock to him.

Singing With the Wounded GIs

We got on board ship, and they pulled the boat from Southampton and on the southern part of England, the southern coast there's the Isle of Wight. And we pulled in and put down our anchor. And we sat on that boat for five days before we moved. And when I was complaining to somebody, they said they were assembling the convoy. It was still wartime, and we came in a convoy. And although our ship was a small ship, it was the *John Ericsson*, we were the largest ship in the convoy, but a convoy could only go the speed of the smaller ships. And occasionally we'd see the destroyers or whoever was guiding us or guarding us when we were coming over, but it took us twenty-three days to get here. And there were no seats on the boat, you know on the deck, very strict. I was in a cabin with five other girls. It was three bunks. [*Points three up high, right/left*]. I got very friendly with one girl. So as I say, we used to walk around the deck. There was nowhere to sit down, but we used to sit on the deck underneath our porthole. And I always take my knitting wherever I go. I would sit there, and I knitted myself a sweater while we were onboard. My girlfriend sitting beside me said, 'Wish I'd thought of bringing my knitting.' She said, 'You have anything I could do?'

I said, 'Yes, I've got more pins, and I've got plenty of yarn. I'm making myself a sweater.'

She made the sleeves for me. We sat there and talked. We got to know each other well. But again, when we had to ride, whether we wanted to or not, we used to sing, my family, my brothers, and I. So I said, 'Let's sing a song.' We'd sing, and we'd be sitting there and there were wounded GIs on board. There were ninety brides, and three of them had babies with them. But there were many, many GIs who were bedridden. We never, ever saw them. They were in the cabins below deck. There were quite a few and they were wounded. One man had lost one arm, but they were walking around and that. They had nowhere to sit down either. So they'd come around and stand there; they'd eventually sit on the ground and we ended up having about thirty or forty of them every day. We'd sit under our porthole, and they'd sit down. And we'd sing, and they'd sing with us, and we taught them a couple of English songs, they taught us a couple of American songs, not the kind you'd sing in church or anything. We had fun and it made it interesting, because they would talk to us, and we would talk to them. I must say that when we were on board, there was one GI that almost lost his arm. He didn't want them to amputate it. He said to me, 'Since I've been in the service and have been abroad, my wife gave birth to our first baby. Could you make something with your knitting?' So, I made them a pair of baby booties, so he could take it. The only thing I knew about him is that he came from Scarsdale. I don't know his name or anything else.

The New York Skyline

In spite of the fact it was twenty-three days, it was March. I got on board ship March the first, and March the twenty-third, we pulled into the New York harbor. And it was raining, and it was foggy, and it was cold. And all of the GIs said, 'You wait until you see the New York skyline. It's the most beautiful skyline in the whole world. Well, we really didn't care about the skyline. It was freezing. It was snowing. It was miserable. I said to the girls, 'I wonder if they had said to us girls, 'Now, if you want to, you can go right around and go back home.'

I said, 'I wonder how many would go.' The thing is, my husband had said, 'You'll probably be put off at Ellis Island.' His sister had written and had told him that she would like me to go and live with her, because I had nobody over here. I knew nobody.

When she had written to the authorities, she said that she would provide a home for me. She had to do that, and she had to give them an estimate of her income, so that they'd know that she could afford to keep me and not throw me out of the house. The Red Cross in New York met the boat and took all the brides to the Red Cross headquarters and interviewed each one of us separately. When it was my turn, they said, 'Where are you going?'

I said, 'Wood-Ridge, New Jersey.'

'Have you made any plans to get there or is somebody going to meet you? How are you expecting to get there?'

I said, 'Well, my husband told me to go to the bus department and get a bus to Journal Square and then Journal Square change and get a bus that would go to Wood-Ridge, which was about twelve miles from Journal Square.'

She said, 'Well, you know exactly where you're going.'

I said, 'I'm going to live with my sister-in-law and her family. And I have a telephone number. And if we call her and if they're home, they'll come and meet us.'

So, the Red Cross lady called the number and said who she was, and they said, 'Oh, yes. We'll be there in about a half an hour.' They let me say hello to her on the telephone. And I waited. Now, a lot of the girls had to go much further, if they were going to California or anywhere else, I mean, they had to go by bus or by train. But it was very easy for me. They came to meet me and took me home. They even brought my mother-in-law.

She lived in Jersey City. So, on their way, they stopped and picked her up. And they had a five-year-old girl, daughter with them. And they picked her up and took me to Wood-Ridge. I was there. It was very, very lovely. They were very, very kind. Of course, I was new, and they showed me around. I can remember the first day when I got there.

'Life in America Was Very Different'

She showed me the house and where the bathroom was and she said, 'Anytime, all you want, go to the bathroom, we have showers and everything.' Well, we didn't have showers in England. We had bathrooms but just with a bath, you know. I think it was the next day. I thought, I'd like to take a bath. But she had said to have a shower. And I thought, well that would be good. So, I walked into the bathroom. She had the most beautiful shower curtain. It was... I've never seen any since that was so pretty. When I got there, I thought, 'Oh, my goodness. I don't want to get this wet.' So, I put it outside the bath and took a shower. Well, I didn't know all of the water was going outside the room. I mopped it up very quickly. It was silly things like that I didn't know, that I never met up with before.

She was very good to me. I actually got a job. Their neighbor was the manager of the telephone company, and I had always wanted to be a telephone operator. And she called me and asked me if I'd like a job and I had nothing to do. I used to help my sister-in-law, and I used to walk her little girl to school every morning, but nothing else really. After the one thing I made such a mess of, I don't think she really wanted me to help them out much. When the chief operator called me, she spoke to me for quite a long time. And then she said, 'Would you like to become a telephone operator? Do you have any questions?'

I said, 'The only thing is, I wonder if they would understand me.' Because this was before the dial. Everything had to be done by voice.

So, she said, 'I'm enjoying this conversation very much.' So anyway, she said, 'Report.'

So, for the first two weeks, they had one supervisor with two students. And for that first two weeks, the first day they made us get acquainted with the board where they had all of these lights, and if any person picked up the telephone, a light would come on. So, you'd pick up this and plug in that light and say, 'Number, please.' And then she'd tell you a number and you pick up the wire. She was in the back one and I was on this one and put in the number. I enjoyed that very much. It was good.

When my husband came home six months later, his mother lived in Jersey City and that's where he lived with her when he came into the Army. So, of course we were going there. So, we moved to Jersey City.

You had to learn how to pronounce that so everybody could understand me because that's how everybody else was saying it. I transferred to the telephone company office in Journal Square. I used to work from five in the evening until eleven o'clock at night, or six to twelve, because you got the same wage and even got a night differential that paid you a little more money, because the young girls didn't want to work at night. They wanted to be able to go on dates, but I couldn't go out on any date. But anyhow, the first day that I went there was a Sunday. They put me between two older operators. They knew I was new to the job. But it worked out. [My life in America] was very, very different.

PART FIVE

THE DISPLACED

"There was an expectancy of a better life; from what we read and heard, we knew that if we were to come to a normal life again, it would be in the United States. It would take time, it would take hard work, but eventually we will be normal living people. That is why I am against war, with every fiber of my body. Because I know what it does to civilian people, primarily mothers with young children... Who is going to take care of them? Nobody cared."

—Child Refugee, World War II

CHAPTER SEVENTEEN

The Refugee

As the world went about its business in the late 1930s, the clouds of war gathered as the policy of appeasement began to bear its terrible fruit. German troops had swallowed all of Czechoslovakia by March 1939; Hitler continued to demand the area known as the Polish Corridor and the outlet to the Baltic Sea at the city of Danzig, which had been lost after World War I. Secretly, he directed his foreign minister to enter into clandestine negotiations with the Soviet Union. Strange fellows bedded down in a 10-year pact of nonaggression, and the secret protocol called for the division of Poland between the Germans and the Soviets, the fascists and the communists. On September 1, 1939, Hitler rolled the dice once more as Germany invaded Poland on false pretenses of Polish aggression. Halina Roman and her family were victims of this division.

Halina was just ten years old, one of six children in her family, five girls and one boy. Halina's grandmother lived with her family and helped take care of all of the children. She attended school in what was the equivalent of present-day grade schools, but by the time Halina was ten years old, in June of 1940 the Russian secret police (NKVD) raided her hometown of Kuligi in northeast Poland. Halina's mother, grandmother, sisters, and brother were evacuated by the Russians to Siberia. After several months of labor in Siberia, Halina and her group of family members embarked on a ten-year odyssey through Uzbekistan, Persia, India, East Africa, finally eventually settling in the United States. However, these travels took their toll on the family, and she lost four of her sisters and her grandmother.

After the long journey full of hunger, fear, and uncertainty, Halina made it to the United States for new opportunities and freedom in February 1951. This interview was recorded by her grandson in 2007, one of my students in the oral history project, at her home in Erie, Pennsylvania, when she was seventy-eight years old.

Halina Roman

I was born on August 28, 1929, in Kuligi, Poland. Kuligi was sort of close to the Russian border. My family consisted of my parents, my grandmother, and my five siblings. I was the oldest. My father was a farmer and we had everything on the farm, all of the animals you could imagine; in Poland at that time the farmers had to be self-sustaining. My father had seasonal help to help him around the place. I remember it was a nice place, we had lots of space. We had gardens, pastures, a river close by, and a couple row boats that you could go fishing in. On top of that my father had a fishery pond where we could just play around. We had a beautiful childhood along with lots of vegetables and food, which was why the beginning was very healthy for us. Then in 1939 when I was just turning ten, the war broke out and everything changed.

Between 1939 and the German invasion of the USSR in 1941, Soviet authorities deported well over a million Poles to the Soviet Union. The exact number unknown; many thousands were murdered in the Katyn Forest and elsewhere. According to the United State Holocaust Memorial Museum, those "branded as 'socially dangerous' and as 'anti-Soviet elements' were forcibly removed from their homes and deported in cattle cars to labor camps in Siberia and Kazakhstan. These civilians included civil servants, local government officials, judges, members of the police force, forest workers, settlers, small farmers, tradesmen, refugees from western Poland, children from summer camps and orphanages, family members of anyone previously arrested, and family members of anyone who escaped abroad or went missing; in most of the camps, all prisoners were expected to work regardless of age or physical condition. Children were in charge of transporting water, gathering firewood, and collecting food. The grueling work and harsh weather often made conditions in the camps unbearable. With little food or medical care, prisoners died every day in large numbers."[14]

Arrest

My father was called into the office in Kuligi on official business because he was the leader of the hamlet of Kuligi. My mother never knew what happened to him, despite the war, and she never did see him again. As much as my mother and I tried, we never found out what happened to my father. Later on, however, we found out that my father was lost in a concentration camp. As for us, my mother, grandmother, and all the rest of the children, I don't know if you would call it arrested, but the NKVD came at six in the morning and pounded on the doors and gave us two hours to pack. This happened in June of 1940. My mother, being as nervous and devastated as she was, packed what she thought was easy to take and could be of value to trade.

Siberia

We were taken to the nearest railroad station, put into cargo cars, and taken to Siberia. The whole trip by train took three weeks, not counting the stoppages. In Siberia we came to a place called Salekhard, which to this day I remember, and it is still on the map. I think today's maps have a lot of names changed. They gave us a house that was abandoned and that's where we lived. While there, my mother became friends with a lady working in an office. By this time it was September or October of 1941. Through my mother's friend, she found out that an agreement had been signed between the Russian and Polish governments. It said that all the Polish people taken to Siberia be relinquished, but they had to travel to South of Russia. My mother got permission to travel, but other than that it was unsupervised and up to my mother how she got to South of Russia, to Kazakhstan. She sometimes had to leave the train to get food for us, which was sometimes not all that easy. In that period of time, I remember suffering from hunger, cold, and needless to say, fear. Fear of strange places and strange people, not to talk about the discomforts. When I watched my mom, I just felt so sorry for her.

I remember my brother Al was only four years old, he was just a baby, and my mother was stuck with all the children. Like all mothers, she only worried about keeping us warm and fed. In route to South of Russia we lost our grandmother, she was close to ninety years old. She got very sick, and my mom admitted her to a hospital, but when my mother went back in a day to see my grandmother, no one could give my mother a clue as to where my grandmother was, or what happened to her. To this day we do not know what happened to her!

'I Do Not Think I Could Find Their Graves'

As we went further south, one by one, we lost all four of my sisters due to malnutrition. There were instances where my mother carried my sisters to the nearest medical facility, but they could not help her. My mother and I had to dig out all the graves, two feet deep. If I could find those sisters who were buried in the hills it would be a miracle. Today even if I had millions of dollars, I do not think I could find their graves. Respectability for the dead was unknown during the war.

We did get south then and by that time there was a Polish army formed under the command of General Anders.[30] The families of these future soldiers of the Polish Army were allowed to leave Russia. My mother accidentally met up with her uncle, who was in the army. We were lucky; of course, at this time there were only three of us: my mother, Al, and myself. We were then put on crowded trains, shoulder to shoulder. Everyone on the train shared because Stalin agreed to give portions of food to soldiers, but not the families. However, the soldiers shared their small portions of mostly canned food with the children. That is how we got out.

Between 1939 and 1941, 1,680,000 Polish people were deported and dispersed all over Russia. We got to the South of Russia, Uzbekistan, and Tashkent was the name of the place. There were a lot of people that got the news about the amnesty; these people were all open, including those candidates for the army. They had to organize all of this, there had to be time for decontamination.

---

[30] *General Anders-* Władysław Anders (1892-1970) was a general in the Polish Army. After the Nazi-Soviet Pact, he was captured by the Soviets but was later turned out to form a Polish Army to fight against the Germans. He also commanded the Polish II Corps in the Allied Italian Campaign, including the nearly impossible capture of German lookout stronghold of Monte Cassino. After the war, he was part of Polish Government in Exile in London.

They had to place the civilian people wherever they could. We lived in just a shack; there was a floor and a mat on the inside of it. Through the roof of the shack, we could see the moon and the stars, and heaven forbid if it rained, we would be wet. I have to say in all honesty, we experienced a lot of sympathy and kindness from a lot of people. The family that let us use their shack asked if we could help them pick their cotton during the day in exchange for food. The food consisted of flat bread, rice, and lots of peppers. I had a very sad experience with the peppers. One time I thought it was salad. I took a mouthful, and I did not know what to do with it.

After this, they took us to the port of Krasnovostsk, where we would travel across the Caspian Sea by an overcrowded old ship. I remember the lines all around the ship just to get to the bathroom. I remember a lot of people in sacks being thrown off the ship because they did not survive. The ship landed in the Port of Pahlevi in Persia, or present-day Iran. Here we had to undergo a disinfection and decontamination process. Then by army trucks, we were taken to Tehran, the capital of Iran.

We stayed in what they called Camp #2, which was made of concrete blocks. These were left over and built by the Germans around the ammunition factory that was there years before. They were surrounded by a brick wall with openings to which we could get to Tehran with permission. While there, I remember that one morning I woke up and could not walk. My mother did her own remedies; she took two hot bricks and put them at the bottom of my feet, and I slept with them on my feet.

The next morning I was able to walk again. We stayed there until August of 1942. By train we then went to another place by the name of Ahwaz where we stayed for eight months. It was a transit point where we had to stay at a hospital because my mother was very sick, and I had typhoid fever. That is why we could not travel any farther because they would not send anyone anywhere unless they were well. They did not want any diseases taken anywhere else.

Then finally we got well, registered again, and through the Persian Gulf and Gulf of Oman we got to Karachi. There we stayed so we could get tested for diseases. We stayed in the army tents, and during the night to go to the bathroom you had to travel up the hills with a lantern. There were desert animals that howled so we had to travel to the bathroom in groups at night.

Then we were put on a big ship under escort across the Indian Ocean to East Africa to Mombasa on November 21, 1942. To give you some statistics, 77,200 left Russia, 33,300 civilians and 15,000 orphans. Those were the lucky ones considering at the beginning 1,680,000 Polish were in Russia. Some went to India, some went to Mexico, and like us some landed in East British Africa. Some of the orphans and civilians went to New Zealand.

The International Organization decided where to put these people by whether there was a certain number of adults that could work, or just children. In East Africa there were twenty-two settlements of camps, not only in the east but in South Africa as well. In each settlement there were 3,500-4,000 people. UNRA, the United Nations Relief and Rehabilitation Administration, were the ones that placed us in the camps. We had Polish school systems in Africa headed by The Ministry of Religious Affairs and the Polish Exile in London. There were 57 schools: 27 elementary, 7 secondary, 13 trade schools and 10 art, music, and craft schools.

Interviewer: Going back to the camps that you were in, could you describe what the conditions were like? What you remember from the camps in Russia, Persia, and East Africa?

The first camp was in Siberia. Salekhard was a city, but it was very small, and we were on the outskirts of it. [31] They assigned us to a very old Russian home with a big wooden stove used to keep warm; we had to burn wood in it. When we got there, I remember the first night. My mother pulled out the sheets and put them on the beds that were just rags rather than mattresses. We woke up in the middle of the night because we were itching and scratching. That place had a lot of bed bugs. We saw them coming down lines on the walls and my mother got the candles out and we started burning them. It took us a week to completely kill off the bugs. There were a lot of fish, and Eskimos were the ones delivering the fish to us. I will never forget when the first Eskimo came to our house, I thought he was an animal; his whole outfit was nothing but fur. He reached into the top of his body and pulled out this fish and he sold it to my mother. My mother bought the fish, but I was petrified of him. My mother used to take me to the store, and she gave this lady some kind of small gift so she would tell us when there would be a delivery of sugar coming to the store. She would say, 'Everyone in line is entitled to a quarter of a kilogram of sugar; if you bring your children, then each one of them is entitled to a quarter of a kilogram of sugar.'

It surprised me to see along the wall of the store what I thought were old branches of wood, but they were Eskimos on sleds being pulled by animals. I realized that they were animals pulling the sled and Eskimos came to the store too. I remember so vividly visiting one of the igloos and the whole place was built with ice with skins of animals inside.

As for the food, I did eat the fish my mother would manage to fry. It was a light trading basis. If my mother had something that

---

[31] *Salekhard*- Russian town on the Arctic Circle, used by the governments of Imperial Russia and the Soviet Union as a prison labor camp; Leon Trosky had been a notable prisoner there.

appealed to someone living there, they would trade. It was a remote area and delivery was of absolute basics. However, if you have a piece of gold, you can get anything. I remember my mother had my grandmother's glasses, which had gold frames. We used the frames and my mother's wedding band for food because that's the only thing that you could trade. We had plenty of wood, it was right next to us. I have recently started to paint, and I have painted a mushroom, a red one. We had plenty of these mushrooms in the nearby woods, which helped us too. My mother cooked them up and I do not know whether these went with fish or not, but they filled an empty stomach. I was young and I did not think much about it, I was not as bad as my mother, who looked ahead.

My mother tried to write letters to Poland to let my father know, but they never got there. Later, we found out that when he got out of wherever he was, he temporarily came home but then the Germans came and sent him to a concentration camp. My aunt was with him, and they never received any of the letters and did not know what happened to us either. There are a lot more details, but generally that is about all I remember from that camp.

Was there any forced labor in that camp?

If you could, my mom would have to go to work every single day in order to get rations of bread: dark, heavy bread. I used to go and help her and of course children were ordered to dig ditches. We landed in Siberia in what they call summertime, which was not as severely cold. It was not warm, but it was not frozen either. Most of us were kids. I do not know what good we did digging ditches, but we threw dirt from one place to another. This camp was only for women and children so they could not get too much out of us.

That camp was out of Russia. It was a place where we waited for our next step in our travels. In Tehran, we were in those cement blocks and literally the insides of them were huge empty spaces. There were no rooms, and it was just like a warehouse. All we got were blankets. We would put the blankets down and there would be two people and next to us there would be a family with a blanket with two or three people. We used to get rations of food and basics. In the community kitchen, we would get soup and tea or coffee. I do not remember much, but I remember the soup was lousy. My mother had my father's suit and traded it to a Persian to get private access to a canteen where she could buy some bread or some wine. We had a sort of dysentery from eating in the community kitchen that we were not used to. Next to us there was a doctor who said, 'Mrs. Kalicki, if you want your children to get out of here, you better get them away from that communal kitchen and put them on tea, wine, and dry bread.'

So that is what my mother fed us for a couple days. We survived and got stronger. That is also the camp where I lost the ability to walk for a brief time, but I got better. My mother and I were not there very long, but then my mother started to get really weak.

Our next stop was Ahwaz and that is where we stayed for eight months. My mother was very sick and there was an English doctor there. He took specific interest in my mother's condition because he had some medicine from England to treat her. She might have known, but I never asked what it was except that she got quite a series of injections. She got better and then I got sick with typhoid fever. That is why we were there for so long.

After examinations again, we finally got to Karachi where the big ocean liner was organized. We were under escort because there was still the threat of bombardment of ships traveling through the Indian Ocean to Mombasa. That was the second camp.

East Africa

Then we got to East Africa. From Mombasa, a port, we traveled by railroad to Kampala, which is the capital of Uganda. From there by truck about ten miles away was a camp by the name of Koja. That was in 1943. It was by Lake Victoria. In that camp we had schools, we had English teachers, we had a cinema, basic medical facilities, and local markets for fresh food. In addition to that we were given very simple types of huts. They were round with banana leaf roofs and beds that were constructed with four pieces of wood with legs, rope, and a mattress. We got nets because there were a lot of mosquitoes there. We were given blouses and pants because in the evening you have to wear those to protect yourself from mosquitoes. I went to school there. We had rations of food given to us such as oil, molasses, but whatever we did get we would separate it. My mom worked in a sewing center to make a little money. We went to markets and got fruit and vegetables. We cooked in very simple outside hotplates. There was a jungle that was not too far away, and on the outskirts, we could pick wild growing bananas, oranges, and potatoes. There were loads of bananas, all sizes. The bananas that you grow here are one kind, yellow. We had varieties of bananas, and the ladies of the evening would sit at the table and play cards and have a whole bunch of bananas. Do you know what passion fruit is? It looks like big plums, but it has a hard outside and on the inside a jelly-like sweet-and-sour taste. I spotted one at a local grocery store and they wanted two dollars for one. I got one, took it home and cut it open, and ate it. I thought how delicious this is! Then my husband Vic says to me, 'You did not save anything for me?' and I said, 'There was only a teaspoon of it all together, buy yourself one!' In Africa, right across the path was a field of passion fruit and I said to myself, if I had that here I could be a millionaire. We had a lot of food available, so we did not have to buy or trade for food. We had school and we had Girl Scouts in the camp. The administration of the camp arranged once in a while for the missionaries to come and they showed us their collection of butterflies.

I myself liked Africa very much. I was there eight years. That is why it came in handy, because when I came to the United States at least I could speak English, book English and not American slang. It was in British Africa, but it was not under British control. It was under control of the United Nations. The British agreed to take these camps because they were British colonies at that time. We had churches and I was in school there. I finished high school and two years' equivalent of college. I also worked as a secretary for priests. I had a lot of friends there too. Maybe that is why I remember because I was young and had friends.

When I came to the United States and married my husband Vic, I would say to him that I did not know anybody, and he knew everyone. At this particular time we had been in Koja for five years. By this time it was also the end of the war, and most of the Polish soldiers [in exile] had by then gone to England. All of the families of these soldiers started moving to our camp, so in the end the people that did not have any intentions of moving camps were moved to a different camp. That is why they moved us to Tengeru, present day Tanzania.

Tanzania

Tengeru at one time was the biggest camp in East Africa; it had four thousand people in it. The days there were very hot. The camp was close to the volcanic lake Duluti and at the foot of Mount Meru, near Mount Kilimanjaro. On any clear day, you could see the snow on the peaks of Kilimanjaro. Meru was closer, but it was a volcanic mountain that was not active anymore. It was a beautiful camp, which was where I worked as a secretary for the three priests. We had a YMCA there where you could go to dance, listen to music, or look at the magazines, and that is where we started to have a little contact with the outside world. My mother then realized that we would have to go somewhere else eventually, and she did not want us to be sent someplace we did not want to go.

To the United States

My mother got in touch with her brother in the United States. My aunt had to send us an invitation and pay for us to come to the United States. My uncle had to sign a guarantee that we would not be a burden to the United States. First, we had to go to Nairobi to go to the American Embassy to go through all sorts of tests so that we would not bring any disease to America. It took a long time, but finally in February 1951 we came to the United States from Mombasa on a merchant boat, back through the Suez Canal, to the Mediterranean, Italy, through Bremen, Germany, and then put on a big ship called the *General S.S. Stargitz*. Then we landed in New York on February 17, 1951. From New York I traveled by train to Erie, Pennsylvania, on February 19. I have been here ever since.

Going back on your experiences throughout your whole trip, what would you say is your most vivid memory of the whole experience?

My most vivid memory is of Africa, my eight years there. Despite the simplicity of life we had there, we also had social life and we were all in the same predicament. We enjoyed and cherished the simplest things, going to church, Girl Scouts, going on picnics, and sometimes we would dare the surroundings because we would go into the edge of the jungle. One time we ran into a wild pig, and we were so petrified we did not know what to do. The poor pig was probably more afraid of us. *[Laughs]* At night we could even hear lions. I enjoyed being in Africa. After Russia and all this traveling through different places, Africa was a sanctuary. We did not have to worry that much, even though there was communist influence and some uprising in tribes in Africa. I liked Africa; my most vivid memory was Africa.

Throughout your whole experience in Europe, you were a child. What did you make of everything at such a young age?

I was only ten. I was thrown out like somebody grabs a little plant, and pulls it out of the dirt and throws it on the ground. I was maybe too young to realize the severity of it. I always thought that my mother would take care of everything. No matter what, she would solve the problem for me. After a while, I realized that it was serious, especially when she was sick. I thought to myself, what would happen if she was gone? Here we are in a strange country with no one to lean on and we knew no one, but she survived and we with her.

'What War Does to Women and Children'

When you reached the United States, was there a sense of relief?

There was an expectancy of a better life, definitely. From what we read and heard, we knew that if we were to come to a normal life again, it would be in the United States. It would take time, it would take hard work, but eventually we will be normal living people. With other people around we will not have fears, we will not have hunger, and we will not have war. That is why I am against war, with every fiber of my body. Because I know what it does to civilian people, primarily mothers with young children. It was devastating and they suffered the most because military men, that is their job. Women and children are not soldiers, they generally suffer hunger, fear, and especially when the government decides that they are going to move people and throw them in God knows where. They did it without any care for the living, which is what they did to us. When they took us away from home, nobody ever gave a thought of how these people are going to make a living. Who is going to take care of them? Nobody cared.

*

I have a little conclusion. I am very proud of you for showing an interest in the events that took place over half a century ago! It disturbed millions of lives, and also caused global turmoil and suffering. It is important to keep up the memory of this horrible last world war and its victims to prevent it from happening again. I lived it as a child who remembers strange places, lots of fear and hunger, and do not forget my parents' devastation in particular, as well as the nations in general. Thank you.

Halina Roman passed away on Independence Day, July 4, 2017, at the age of 87.

CHAPTER EIGHTEEN

The German Schoolgirl

The Great Depression was plunging not only the United States but the entire world into new depths. In 1932, just as in America, a brand-new government was voted into power in Germany; here, though, mainstream politicians lay down with a populist upstart party that pushed a platform of vague and sinister promises to redress grievances and solve Germany's economic and political woes.

Eva Koenig was born in 1926 in eastern Germany in the state of Silesia just twenty miles from the Polish border. Only 13 years old at the start of the war, she lived with her older sister and parents in a little town, where they owned and operated an inn. In January 1945, everyone east of the Oder River was evacuated, including her family. Fearing the Russian advance from the east, Eva and her sister, who was eight months pregnant at the time, began to make their way to western Germany where the family of Eva's brother-in-law lived. The two sisters then began a trek that would take four days and four nights. Although her mother was still living with them at the time, she headed toward Breslau in an attempt to find their father, who had recently become a prisoner of war of the Russians.

After the war, Eva remained in West Germany until she came to the United States; after arriving in the country, she went to Vermont. This interview was conducted in 2006 for our oral history project when she was eighty years old.

Eva Koenig

I was born in eastern Germany on March 31, 1926, and moved to the United States in 1958. The war in Germany started in 1939, and I was 13 years old.

[Before the war], the economy was very bad, people were without work, we had a lot of unrest and people were hoping that someone would come and help us out of the misery.

I had heard [about the hyperinflation that happened around the early 1920s] from my parents. It must've been terrible, they would make a million dollars in one day in their business, and then the next day when they went to the bank, they got maybe a few dollars for it.

[The Great Depression] was all over the world, depression, hunger, unemployment. Before Adolf Hitler came to power, there were two [types of people]: people who wanted him, because he promised work and jobs for everyone, and others who saw that he might not be so good for us. I did not really feel it personally so much; I was young.

In the big cities, [politics] did divide people, yes, to where there were actually fights by both parties against each other. When the war started, just like in this country, people tried to get together and say that 'we have to stand behind the elected president.' But deep down many of the elder ones, especially my parents and grandparents, feared that it would not come to a good end.

Many tried to stand behind [Hitler] because he was in charge of the troops, he was in charge of everything, and they were still hoping he would do good, because in those six years as chancellor, he had done a lot of good, he did find good jobs for those people. He built factories, he had people working. It looked like it could be getting better and better [for the] economy, but other people were not so happy with him; because he was a dictator, they felt that the leadership wasn't that good for the country. If anybody spoke openly against the war, they probably were incarcerated. I was very young; some talked about it among themselves. You'd hear it in families when just the family was together with good friends. They would have discussions about it, and arguments, but not in public.

The summertime 1936 Berlin Olympic Games were used for propaganda purposes, the unveiling of the concept of a master race and the showcasing of German might and militarism. An international boycott effort failed; Hitler's leadership and Germany's prestige was confirmed in the eyes of many at home and abroad.

I don't know if the 1936 Olympics in Berlin were really an accomplishment for the country, but it proved that he did something in all those years that he was president/chancellor. For the three years [prior] he had the use of the street, there were no trucks or anything like that, but [with] offenders of any kind, they would disappear; we often didn't know what happened to them. And whoever was out, they would learn how to do good things. We were actually in groups, and the girls and boys were separated. We did handicrafts. [Hitler] had organized something similar to the Brownies here, [Girls Scouts and Boy Scouts], one for the boys and one for the girls. That was the same, we met once a week in the afternoon and did different things. We had a leader, which was in our case a girl, who was maybe five years older than we were. She taught us all kinds of things, handicrafts. We helped the farmers in the summertime, and we went to elderly people and helped them. That's what we did in our small town. In the big cities it might have been a little bit more on the political side. We sung together, went to concerts together. Like I said, it was not political in our town.

'Our War Started'

It was 1939 when our war started. That's when the soldiers marched through our town, toward the border, and that's when the sad, sad part started. [We lived close to the Polish border]; quite close, we were twenty-five kilometers, which is less than twenty miles, but [before the war], nobody bothered us because there were very tight borders.

In the beginning, it was not very much for me as a child, because I was still in school. But what the girls in our youth group did now, when we got together, was that we started to knit for the soldiers, because some of them were in Poland and later in Russia. So we knitted scarves and mittens for them, things like that. We'd send packages; send letters to those who didn't have any family. Otherwise, of course, we had food stamps and a lot of things were not very easy to come by, because the factories were all changed into places where we made equipment for the war. We had our own business, so both of my parents worked in the business and so did I after I got out of school. All available women, unless they had a lot of children, they had to go to factories.

I had no 'teen years'; there were no dances or get-togethers. There was a movie once in a while, but it was a very sheltered life, really. We sat together in the evening, maybe reading or doing handicrafts, but there was no television. That was just the life; whether that was just because of the war, I'm not sure. Maybe I

could only see the difference afterwards more than at the time because that was just life for me as a child.

Was there a lot of support for the troops? Oh, yes, naturally,
because they were everybody's brother, father, son, so naturally
we supported them. I didn't know of anybody who [vocally opposed the war, or who did not offer troop support.] And again,
they probably would not have stayed on the streets [very long], or
wherever they said it. They would have disappeared, because that's
what they did, under dictatorship.

For the elder generation, people who were really involved in
politics, I guess they saw [the war] coming. I personally did not.
My father was very opposed to the whole politics of those days,
and I remember that my mother often had to warn him to be qui-
et, not to talk too loud, when he spoke against it all.

After the years passed by into the war, city bombardment started up from the English. That is when we were fortunate to be in
the east, because they never came to the east [at that time]; I guess
it was too far to fly. [Then] only the western part of Germany was
bombarded, so we didn't hear or see any of those terrible things.
Soon when some of the cities were very much bombarded and
they didn't even have enough housing for those people who had
lost everything, they were starting to send those people to the east
part of Germany, and we had to take those westerners into our
home, so that they would have a home. We had one woman with
a child, a school child, I don't remember her age.

*Student interviewer: Did you know anyone who was living in the
west?*

My sister got married in 1944 and her in-laws lived in the west.
But it was also in a smaller town, so there was really nothing to
bombard because it was just people living there. But later on they

started, it wasn't too bad there. We had relatives in Berlin, the capital of Germany. They brought a lot of their valuables to us actually because they didn't know what would happen there, but they were able to go to some other relatives nearby who were on the outskirts of Berlin, so they did not come to the east.

Some teachers might have talked about [the war] to us, about politics even. I had heard most of it through my parents, though, and like I said, from the radio and newspaper. For the teachers there maybe also was a little bit of worry; in case they said too much, it would hurt them. They might be taken off the job if they were saying anything against the regime.

*

My sister's husband was in the war, from the beginning to the end, wounded twice. We didn't have a big family, but I had two cousins who were drafted in 1940 or '41. And my father had to go in 1945, just a few months before the war ended. They drafted all available men in town, and even young boys. They had to go defend the capital of our state, Silesia, which is called Breslau. It's now Polish; after the war this whole part became Polish. He was fifty years old at the time, a World War I veteran. He felt terrible about it, he was very much opposed. But of course, he had to go; like most soldiers do when they are called to fight for the country, they go. It was very hard for him. He was a prisoner of war of the Russians, but since he was old and not very well health-wise they did not take him to Russia, they kept him in Poland, near Silesia actually, in a camp for just about three or four months and then they sent him home. He was not treated too badly.

'A Very Hard Time'

Before the war ended, that was really the worst part for us. We had to leave our home and house and flee that whole area because the Russians were coming from that side, naturally, and that was the worst part. We packed one suitcase each and we hoped to be back in a couple of weeks, once the war was over. That never happened because the Russians occupied that part, and from then on, Germany was divided.

We found shelter in that small town where my brother-in-law's relatives lived, and we had to start a new life all together. So that was very hard, and at that time there was really no food at all because like I said we had to go to the west, and the west was bombed out. So that was a very hard time.

'The Russians Were Reaching the Border'

Through some people who had to do with the government in our town, [we learned that the Russians were reaching the border]. They heard it, and they knew that our town would have to be evacuated. So they forwarded it to us, and in the morning at seven o'clock, we had to all leave. Since one of our relatives and neighbors was part of that town hall meeting, he came that night when he returned from the meeting. He came at twelve o'clock and informed us. So we had until seven o'clock in the morning. My father had already been drafted before that a couple of months earlier, so I was just with my mother and my older sister. My older sister was eight months pregnant. My mother decided not to go with us; she wanted to go in the direction where she knew my father would be, just somehow hoping to be able to help him. So my sister and I were the ones who actually went on a trek, they called it. Just trucks or whatever they had, horses and wagons, they put us on them so that we could leave the town. In our town there were no more trains leaving. We had some buses, but there was nothing coming. Everybody knew the Russians were close to the border because we could hear their cannons, so we wanted to go at that time because everybody was afraid of the Russians.

Difficult Journey

It was very difficult traveling with my sister with her advanced state of pregnancy; she was healthy, but the problem was that we had to go to the city, which would have taken us under normal circumstances maybe eight to ten hours per train, changing a few times on the way. It took us four days and four nights. Because there were hardly any trains going, sometimes we had to wait somewhere for hours and hours until something came. Try as we were able, the Red Cross was still working so they helped us because of my sister. They had blankets there, and some oatmeal for us to eat. Otherwise, there were no restaurants or anything for us to go into. Of course my mother packed both of us a knapsack we had on our backs, so we had food and water.

'We Left Everything'

We had to leave behind everything; we had a large house in which we rented apartments upstairs. So we left everything, we just had one suitcase, whatever we could carry, and my mother locked up the house hoping we would come back, but we never did. So we had to leave everything.

My sister was still living with us because her husband was in Russia at the time, so we were going to her in-laws. No, they did not know, because we had no way of getting in touch with them. Now, they had heard on the radio in the meantime that all of eastern Germany was evacuated, so they expected us, they didn't know when, but they had expected us. Quite a few houses [had been destroyed], but their house was on the outskirts of town, so that near there, there was no bombardment, [although the town was being bombed when we were there]. Every house during the war had to have one part of the cellar made stable enough, and emergency food had to be in there where the people who lived there could stay wherever there was bombardment. First the sirens would go off, terrible, through the whole town, drive you crazy and everybody was running across the street or wherever they would have to go—everybody knew where they would have to go in a shelter. The people were running with a few things in their arms, with their children in their arms, just to get there. Sometimes, of course, the bombs would come before they had even reached the shelter, but it was tough.

We had to sit in the shelter until there was a siren going again, telling us that it was clear, which sometimes could have been up to ten hours. So that was pretty scary. [At times this happened] maybe twice a week, it was not too much; like I said, this was a small town with no military there, or factories. Sometimes they'd just swoop a bomb down on the way home from the big cities when they had something left over. We stayed in this town from February until May 1945, when the war ended.

*

My mother and father were very close; my mother knew that my father was not too well. So I guess it was just natural instinct, but of course they would never let her into that city, so they told her to leave. The whole city was closed, and nobody could come in or go out anymore. We tried to protect it from the Russians but were unable to. For a few weeks and months, they did try to defend it, and it was completely destroyed because of it. She found a train and a few days after we had arrived, she came too. People were very much afraid of the Russians because they had heard so many bad stories of them, raping women, stealing and murdering, so there was great fear.

When we came close to the end of the war, we all got together, our small family, and we said, 'If we ever have to leave here, we will meet in that particular town.' And he was released in September from the Russians, and came right there, to that town.

My sister's husband was wounded again at the very end of it, and then he was okay. He still wanted to go and help, but gratefully he didn't have to fight against the Russians then, but against the English, then later Americans. Of course it was much easier for him because he was also a prisoner of war [in the west]; I cannot say for sure now if it was English or American, but they didn't keep him very long, and then he was released.

I mean during the war I can't really say [how most Germans view the British]; I guess that most Germans found them as the enemy because they were bombarding our land. We all knew that our politicians had started the war, but it's just very difficult because you don't know whom to believe and what to believe.

But definitely, [the western allies] were much more humane to prisoners of war, or even in our case, when the English and the Americans together came in our town, they were very kind to us civilian people. They even gave us something to eat when they had something. I mean, there was no question about it, decent. Oh, we were not scared anymore, we felt that that was the end; it couldn't get any worse than it was.

'There was No One Else to Blame'

Were you relieved that the war was over?

Yes, oh definitely.

By that point had most of the pride of fighting subsided and were the people getting sick of fighting?

Oh, [most Germans] had gotten sick of the war a long time ago. Everybody knew it was impossible to do what our chancellor wanted us to do, to more or less conquer the whole world. Therefore, we wanted it to end earlier. Many of the officers close to him wanted to end it, and tried to assassinate him, but it was not successful, unfortunately. They put bombs next to him and all kinds of things and he for some reason was never hurt. Then of course he went on the radio and made a big speech that 'nobody can harm me,' and all that. For us, we all hoped that somebody would finally be successful, but nobody was, and we had to just struggle along.

It was a long war, from 1939 until 1945, so I would say 1941, 1942, most people [were thinking], 'let's stop it.' But they couldn't say it out loud, but everyone hoped it would end somehow.

Hitler was a good speaker, but that was just for the ones who liked him. [*Chuckles*] You can make a good speech and still not say what they [the civilians] wanted to hear, and he'd tell them he didn't want to hear what they said. So you'd listen too; as long as the war hadn't ended, he had nothing else to say to us that we wanted to hear. In the end, actually, we didn't hear much from him or about him. He was in Berlin, and of course the Russians were coming from one side, the English and Americans from the other side, and finally, of course, he took his own life.

Was Hitler blamed for the war after it was over?

From the very beginning he was blamed. There was no one else to blame. He had a good propaganda minister there.

Did people realize that it was propaganda, or did they go along with it?

Well as always, different people have different impressions and ideas. Some saw it as if he said so it has to be good, it has to be right, and this was great and wonderful, and they went along with it. Then there were others who thought it was impossible what he promised. There were always two people and I think it was probably [split] fifty-fifty.

Did you hear any news about what was happening, as far as the Jewish people?

Yes. That's a story all by itself, a terrible story. I guess we didn't hear too much during the war, because it was so terrible, and he knew it. He knew that people wouldn't like it. So except for the propaganda which said the Jews were all bad, that's what they tried to tell us, which we knew they were not because we had friends who were Jews, we went to school with Jewish people, had businesses with Jews. So we certainly did not have that impression, but that was what was told to us: they are all bad. The synagogues were burned down, that was the terrible part of the Hitler Regime.

How did you feel when [you were told] that the Jews were supposedly bad, yet you had known so many?

It was unbelievable for us, because like I said, they were very good people. But there was nothing we could do.

What happened to your family after the war?

It was a slow start. I lived with my mother in one room; when my father came, he joined us. Then, after a couple of months, I had found a job as a maid with a business family where I could work and also have a small home where I could sleep. That started to be my home. We stayed in the west because we could never go back to the east.

Rebuilding After the War

They started rebuilding pretty quickly afterwards. Rebuilding after the war was very difficult, of course; what they did, especially in the large cities, since most of our houses are built out of bricks, not wood, they cleaned the bricks from all of the houses that had fallen down and rebuilt with those old bricks until they got new supplies, which took quite a while. They built shelters, of course, that everybody could stay in. And again, everybody had the house full, sheltering neighbors or relatives from another town. It was a few tough years after the war. I must say this is what we learned after the war. Everybody worked wherever it was needed. I remember we, as young girls, in our free time were taken to a place not too far from us with trucks, and they would get, I don't know what it's called now, but it was material to burn because we didn't have enough coal, we didn't have enough wood. But they could go into the earth, the people who knew about it, and they cut it in bricks. We young girls, we had to take it out and put it up on the trucks and carry it from one place to another. So that would be driven down and brought into the city and given to people, so that whoever didn't have anything to burn because it was cold, would burn this. It was not coal but as hard as coal, and I don't even know if it exists here in this country, but it was a form of heating the houses.

It took, I would say, until 1948 for things to get back to 'normal.' We had a new chancellor and good politicians; of course,

Adenauer was our first one. In 1948 they brought new money, a complete change in the money, so we lost everything we had in the bank, but we started with new money. For some reason, we were able at this time with new money to buy a few things, but before that there was hardly anything that we had in those three years from '45 to '48. Everything was really down and that's how long it took. In those three years we didn't go anywhere, we couldn't do anything, just trying to rebuild and working to get something for ourselves, whatever we could for ourselves to survive. Do any job which came along and help out wherever we could.

Of course the Americans helped the Germans after the war. What was it called now? One of the generals or presidents sent food over; we got a lot of help from the Americans.[32] They came with planes, especially to Berlin, which was encircled by Russians, and they sent planes to drop food. Actually, we as a family, they found contacts for us through the churches, and a family from Vermont started to send us packages, which was very nice. When I came to the United States, they were the first people I met. [*Long pause*] It was wonderful to get those packages with clothes for us and food. [*She cries.*] Every few months we received them, and soon, they started to write letters. They'd put a letter in English, and we found somebody in Germany who could translate it. Then my father would answer them in German. Those Vermont people had neighbors who spoke German and who translated for them. It became a close friendship.

---

[32] *we got a lot of help from the Americans-* The European Recovery Act, nicknamed the Marshall Plan after its chief architect, Secretary of State George C. Marshall, which provided 12.5 billion dollars for post-war recovery.

Eva H. Koenig passed away on February 4, 2018, in Germany, having moved back to be with family after her husband died.

CHAPTER NINETEEN

The Holocaust Survivor

Whenever I look at the photos sent to my uncle before the war, I experience the same surge of feelings—pain, sadness, and great pity. I hurt because we all look so young, yet nobody survived except myself. Our family was one of hundreds of thousands whose fate was the same. Thousands of little children with potential for greatness in many fields perished.

Before the war, Poland had the greatest concentration of Jews with active writers, painters, musicians, and teachers. We were a community with high moral values, vibrant with cultural activities: newspapers, theaters, activities, and a variety of political parties.

[Following the war], the Warsaw ghetto was a huge, leveled, empty place. The skeletons of burned buildings and people are bulldozed into the ground. No one would guess what was once here. The people who died knew well they were not dying for a cause; most did not have the luxury of defending themselves. They were destroyed just for being Jews in the wrong place and time. All, without exception, asked to be remembered. We, who accidentally survived, owe them to keep their memories alive. As the Bible says: When a person dies, it is as if a whole world died because we carry within us a whole world.[15]

—Lily Muller, Memoirs

Lily Muller visited our high school on a few occasions to witness the reunions we hosted with World War II liberators and Holocaust survivors, as detailed in my 2016 book, A Train Near Magdeburg. *Indeed, her husband Oscar had been liberated on that train. In December 2007, one of my students visited with her at her home, when she was eighty-five years of age.*

Lily Muller

I was born in Lodz, the second biggest city in Poland, December 2, 1922. It was an industrial city; I was there until I was sixteen years old. I had a normal, wonderful life with my parents and my two brothers. I was going to a private school, which I loved, because the teachers were very close to the pupils, and I was doing well in school; I enjoyed school. We knew a lot of what was going on because my parents had a bookstore, and having a bookstore they got a lot of information from other things, and I myself saw a book printed in Germany which showed a photograph of people in camps, so [some of] the Germans themselves did not like their world view. Actually Mr. Hitler decided to put them there, to probably make them a little more to his liking. So, we knew that Europe was heading to a war, and we Jews would be very vulnerable.

In the meantime, we had in our bookstore windows all possible books printed against Hitler. When the time was near for them to come to Lodz, we had to take all those books and bring them to the house, and still in warm weather, burn those books; my parents, having lived through the First World War, had a very bad time then, there was hunger, and they knew we were not safe. I knew what it was going to be—not exactly, of course, [because if we knew what was going to happen], maybe we would have gone to the United States, where we had family. But I remember this book episode, because in history we ourselves read about things which happened previously to people who were not going along with the regime. We certainly did not [go along] ...

The Arrival of the Germans

The first of September, 1939, the Germans came into my town. A lot of Deutsche Polen, who were [of German extraction] and who had lived in Poland for many years, they were still German-oriented, they lined the streets—the German soldiers were bleeding, very heavily. Our town now changed completely because you could not be in the street. [Some] Jews were called in and made to dance in front of the Germans, who had a lot of fun, and who photographed it [for sport].

The schools were then closed completely. My uncle, who was part of the city government, had to hide in my aunt's apartment. It was just an awful time. Our store was closed, and we lost it; we did not own it anymore. I did not know how to deal with it, especially because my father and my brother went to Warsaw, because they thought that Warsaw would be spared. But there was such shooting on the streets in Warsaw, and there was no food, so he came home, and we were relieved very much that he was home. This had been going on for a long time and we found out that this particular city would be incorporated into the Reich. The family decided to contact some people my father had business with in Warsaw and asked them if we could go there, if they could help us find some lodging. Pretty soon part of the family went there, but my father did not want to make my mother sleep in one room like they put a few families because everybody was coming to Warsaw.

Before World War II, Warsaw was the epicenter of Jewish life and culture in Poland; 350,000 Jews made up its prewar population. This vibrant Jewish community was the largest in both Poland and Europe, and was the second largest in the world, second only to New York City.[16]

She [my mother] was supposed to wait for another opportunity to come a little later. It was very difficult there too, although we were not so scared because in our town, they were already talking about making a ghetto and closing it, whereas in Warsaw it was a few years until that happened. But of course, I worked because I had no school. I decided to open like a little kindergarten for the children of older women who were working; I think it was a good thing to do. But slowly I started work and saved change; my father opened a little library there, which I took care of. He found ways also to make some money so we could have some food to eat. It was hard, the people lived in one room, there was no food. You could buy food on the black market. Little boys used to bring the food from out of Warsaw city and where the war was surrounding us; the little boys used to put out bricks and put the food there and somehow get money for it. But many of them died, because when the Germans saw that somebody was doing it, they killed them. They did not care about killing people, it was just they really treated people as things. Food, I do not even remember what food we ate; we did not have much.

The Warsaw Ghetto

The Warsaw Ghetto was famous for hunger and for terrible sickness. A lot of people were sick from typhus, and a lot of people were just simply dying from hunger, a lot of children especially, all over the street. The next day you would not see them anymore; in the morning a little wagon would pick up all those people and take them to the cemetery. The people who still had money could maybe eventually save themselves, but generally it was very bad. The Germans had a way of killing the Jews. First, they started with little things, taking away all your coats, took away all your radios, you did not have anything that reminded you that you were a human being. I was lucky because when I was in the underground, I had to bring bulletins from the radio, and because of that I knew what was going on, but otherwise, people did not really know.

Lily was able to slip out and smuggle food and munitions in to the ghetto fighters, she also worked to clean guns and create Molotov cocktails.

The Ghetto Uprising

As 1943 dawned, the SS returned to the ghetto for another major deportation. They encountered the first armed resistance from the ghetto fighters and beat a hasty retreat, leaving behind wounded and weapons, and temporarily called off the operation. For the next three months, the ghetto fighters organized and prepared for the final struggle. On the eve of Passover, April 19, the Germans returned again, this time with the aim of liquidating the ghetto once and for all, in time for Hitler's birthday on the 20th. By then, there were between 300-350 active fighters; the young were now the real leaders of the ghetto, having decided not between life and death, but rather, how to die.[33]

The Warsaw Ghetto was destroyed in 1943 when the Germans decided to [liquidate the ghetto], but before this even happened I worked for the Jewish underground, because I was promised I was

---

[33] *By then, there were between 300-350 fighters-* Bauer, Yehuda. '*Current Issues in Holocaust Education and Research: The Unprecedentedness of the Holocaust in an Age of Genocide.*' Lecture notes, International School for Holocaust Studies at Yad Vashem, Jerusalem, Israel. July 21, 2016.

going to get the first papers from my friend. They were [identity] papers taken from dead people that were brought in from the Russian side that would verify [if this person was alive or dead]. So, they took these papers from dead people and [had us assume those identities], and then you could then go out of Warsaw and be out of the ghetto, if you had what they called a good face, that means a little wide, light, and you were could speak well, people survived on those papers.

At one time when things were bad, I decided to speak to my parents; we were in this camp together. I tried it; the first time when I tried it, it did not work out, but the second time I left this place. I was scared because you know our faces were very sad and it was very hard to always remember you are [supposed to be] very happy.

I knew when [the Germans] were planning to burn the ghetto; I went out just in time.

*

The 1944 Polish Warsaw Uprising lasted for 63 days was initiated by the underground Polish Home Army to coincide with the Soviet advance, but the Red Army treacherously halted on the outskirts of Warsaw and allowed the German Army to suppress it, the goal being to eliminate Polish resistance to Soviet rule after the war ended. When that uprising, the largest in World War II, was over, the Germans forced civilian survivors to move. Wither her Aryan papers, Lily was sent to Germany.

I was there at the time of the [1944] Polish Uprising where everybody had to leave Warsaw. But the Germans sent us to Germany; they needed people to work in their factories.

Berlin

Unfortunately, they sent me to Berlin, where I was for over a year. Berlin was bombed twice a day, once by the English and once by the Americans. We had to go to a shelter so we did not show any signs of lights to the planes; every night we suffered through this, it was very hard. Eventually our factory was bombed and there was no more work for us. So, we were really afraid this was very bad for us, because first of all we were already depleted and were not fed very well because it was a very bad camp, it was very dangerous. I remember we asked a German whose older son had already died, it was toward the end, and she spoke to the boss, who was manufacturing caskets for the military. So we went there, and luckily for us, he took us.

I was afraid also of the Polish [slave workers] also in this camp because, you know, people started to become friendly, and some of them did not like the Jews, so I was not happy there. We could go down to Berlin, and in the end, [due to Allied bombing, we could not recognize any streets.

We were very lucky; there was a room of thirty people where there were all types of people. We also knew a little German, which was a little helpful. Where we washed ourselves there was only cold water and there were actually icicles hanging off the ceiling, but you learn how to adjust to it; that was something we could live with. When we went to our factories, they had showers for the men, so we used to go there very quickly and shower, dress, and go out, so we had a shower once in a while. Listen, this was no Auschwitz, but these six years of this terrible hunger and fear, I think that it took its toll on us.

'No One Survived From My Family'

I had two brothers. My brother went back to my town because my mother had an opportunity to come to Warsaw; we smuggled ourselves to Warsaw. I still think maybe if we would be together, we could have done something in Warsaw, but they were awful.

No one survived from my family. We were five people and we had grandparents on both sides, no one survived. My two friends, maybe more, from my schools survived, but my family, no.

'I Wanted to Live'

Student interviewer: What kept you going during the Holocaust, to keep pushing through and wanting to survive?

The fact that I was young. I wanted to live, and besides that, I wanted somebody to survive to tell the truth about what happened, because if Hitler would have won, there would be no humanity, no civilization. I knew in my bones that people have to prove that there is still humanity.

[After the war ended], they sent us to Brussels and we were very lucky we were there because there were already international aid groups. They also registered us with the city so we could get coupons for food; there was an international committee that started to take names and ask where you wanted to go. It took me five years only to come to the United States, can you believe this? [Laughs]

Have you ever gone back to Poland?

Yes. I went twice. My father had a house there and I wanted to take a little time to see it. I wanted to go to my room of our apartment; my heart was beating, and I went up there, I rang the bell, and the woman asked me what I wanted. I said, 'This apartment looks exactly like the one when we left. Our piano, the furniture, the pictures on the wall, everything.' I said, 'May I have one little picture, and she said, 'No, it is not yours!' Those people thought that they were entitled to it; of course it is hard. My friend, who was a pianist, went down to his apartment. He went there after the war because he survived, and they did not want to give him the piano. So, some people took advantage. [But] the biggest loss was the family, you know. I was still young when I left, I was sixteen when I did not see my mother anymore. Then gradually I lost everyone. I was still young, I do not know how to say whether we were less independent from the parents, but the families were very tight in Europe, like maybe sometimes you see here, Italian families who are very close to each other. That was characteristic of the Europeans.

*

I met my husband in Belgium. He came there from a camp, I never would have met him otherwise [laughs] because he was with the Russians later on, because this part was all east, so it touches where Ukraine is now. In Europe, every country after a few years changed their borders because of the wars. There were wars very often; they did this like a game of chess, and that is how it really was.

I found this work in a consulate; it was hard for me because I had to speak German, and French, and Polish, because it was a Polish consulate. But I did not know French, I knew German and Polish; I really raced to get to know this language that I should be able to speak with French people, but the learning process was very hard. I learned the French fast, then I started to learn English, because I wanted to come here.

To the United States

[When I came to the United States], I was living in Long Beach, New York; we lived there for fourteen years. You could go into New York in about an hour. I was working, making dresses to order, I was doing alterations, because that was easy. I did not have to learn anything. But this is also a war tragedy; I did not have a chance to go to college, and I had to work right away for myself. I could not pay for college, so I never went to college. I remember before the war, they planned for me, because I knew what I wanted for myself. I wanted a career. I wanted to be educated, but I made peace with myself about this. But I used to take different small courses, a few each year, each semester. I think that what I learned from it, that you can do a lot for yourself by studying, by reading a lot, by just being interested.

'I Know What War Is'

All I can tell you is, I am hoping there will be peace because I know what war is. I do not see much hope for it. I am eighty-five, I do not have much more to live. I was hoping people would learn from all this disaster. I am lucky my son did not get into the Vietnam War. We went marching and we were trying, and he is well educated, and my daughter is well educated; those were my goals. I have such wonderful visitors, and I admire you, too, for doing this job. Maybe somebody will find out that war is really horrible. Maybe they will do something about it.

Lily Muller passed away on December 2, 2015, at the age of 93.

To Keep Them With Us

In revisiting these stories, I came to realize that they are no less important than my previous books' tales of combat and sacrifice; in fact, they offer us a hidden facet of the story of World War II that is often overlooked. And these narratives were not easy to dig up; the simple fact was, many of the participants, until the sunset of their lives, had never spoken about their personal histories. Who cared to listen? They were frankly hard for me to find in the archives, but then again, I have a confession of sorts to make—I suppose my own biases and interests for the combat veteran narratives in the collecting phase took precedence. Although I never discouraged any student in our oral history project from talking to a civilian who lived through World War II, I just didn't emphasize that necessity at the time. Going through and researching and fleshing out the narratives, I realize how important these stories really are, and I'm proud of the ones who gathered them, many of them now the parents of their own high school age children.

Many of my readers, most of them children of the World War II generation, have written to me, or commented on my social media posts, remarking on how little their parents told them about their experiences during the war; they are thankful for the opportunity to immerse themselves in these recollections that must ring familiar to those of their parents, unlocking perhaps a mystery or two behind an unopened door. It is my hope that this volume of the series has in a small way rounded out another part of that story, and that in reading or listening to these late-in-life remembrances, we help to keep them alive, learning anew about the sacrifices they made for their families, and the world.

We honor their legacy by remembering their stories. We keep them close. We say their names.

*

IF YOU LIKED THIS BOOK, you'll love hearing more from the World War II generation in my other books. On the following pages you can see some samples, and I can let you know as soon as the new books are out and offer you exclusive discounts on some material. Just sign up at matthewrozellbooks.com

Some of my readers may like to know that all of my books are **directly available from the author, with collector's sets which can be autographed** in paperback and hardcover. They are popular gifts for that 'hard-to-buy-for' guy or gal on your list. Visit my shop at matthewrozellbooks.com for details.

THE THINGS OUR FATHERS SAW ® SERIES:

VOICES OF THE PACIFIC THEATER

WAR IN THE AIR: GREAT DEPRESSION TO COMBAT

WAR IN THE AIR: COMBAT, CAPTIVITY, REUNION

UP THE BLOODY BOOT-THE WAR IN ITALY

D-DAY AND BEYOND

THE BULGE AND BEYOND

ACROSS THE RHINE

ON TO TOKYO

HOMEFRONT/WOMEN AT WAR

CHINA, BURMA, INDIA

ALSO: A TRAIN NEAR MAGDEBURG

ABOUT THE AUTHOR

Photo Credit: Joan K. Lentini; May 2017.

Matthew Rozell is an award-winning history teacher, author, speaker, and blogger on the topic of the most cataclysmic events in the history of mankind—World War II and the Holocaust. Rozell has been featured as the 'ABC World News Person of the Week' and has had his work as a teacher filmed for the CBS Evening News, NBC Learn, the Israeli Broadcast Authority, the United States Holocaust Memorial Museum, and the New York State United Teachers. He writes on the power of teaching and the importance of the study of history at TeachingHistoryMatters.com, and you can 'Like' his Facebook author page at AuthorMatthewRozell for updates.

Mr. Rozell is a sought-after speaker on World War II, the Holocaust, and history education, motivating and inspiring his audiences with the lessons of the past. Visit MatthewRozell.com for availability/details.

About this Book/

Acknowledgements

*

A note on historiographical style and convention: to enhance accuracy, consistency, and readability, I corrected punctuation and spelling and sometimes even place names, but only after extensive research. I did take the liberty of occasionally condensing the speaker's voice, eliminating side tangents or incidental information not relevant to the matter at hand. Sometimes two or more interviews with the same person were combined for readability and narrative flow. All of the words of the subjects, however, are essentially their own.

Additionally, I chose to utilize footnotes and endnotes where I deemed them appropriate, directing readers who wish to learn more to my sources, notes, and side commentary. I hope that they do not detract from the flow of the narrative.

First, I wish to acknowledge the hundreds of students who passed through my classes and who forged the bonds with the World War II generation. I promised you these books someday, and now that many of you are yourselves parents, you can tell your children this book is for them. Who says young people are indifferent to the past? Here is evidence to the contrary.

The Hudson Falls Central School District and my former colleagues have my deep appreciation for supporting this endeavor and recognizing its significance throughout the years.

Cara Quinlan's sharp proofing and suggestions helped to clean up the original manuscript.

Naturally this work would not have been possible had it not been for the willingness of the veterans to share their stories for posterity. All of the veterans who were interviewed for this book had the foresight to complete release forms granting access to their stories, and for us to share the information with the New York State Military Museum's Veterans Oral History Project, where copies of the original interviews reside. Wayne Clarke and Mike Russert of the NYSMMVOP were instrumental in cultivating this relationship with my classes over the years and are responsible for some of the interviews in this book as well. Please see the 'Source Notes.'

I would be remiss if I did not recall the profound influence of my late mother and father, Mary and Tony Rozell, both cutting-edge educators and proud early supporters of my career. To my younger siblings Mary, Ned, Nora, and Drew, all accomplished writers and authors, thank you for your encouragement as well. Final and deepest appreciations go to my wife Laura and our children, Emma, Ned, and Mary. Thank you for indulging the old man as he attempted to bring to life the stories he collected as a young one.

NOTES

Source Notes: **Helen Quirini.** Interviewed by Michael Russert and Wayne Clarke, August 31, 2004. Latham, NY. Deposited at NYS Military Museum.

Source Notes: **Mabel Colyer, Frances Cooke, Ethel Severinghaus.** Interviewed by Michael Russert and Wayne Clarke, August 6, 2003. Deposited at NYS Military Museum.

Source Notes: **Ruth A. Bull.** Interviewed by Michael Russert and Wayne Clarke, May 19, 2003. Amsterdam, NY. Deposited at NYS Military Museum.

Source Notes: **Leonard Amborski.** Interviewed by Michael Russert and Wayne Clarke, May 6, 2008. Buffalo, NY. Deposited at NYS Military Museum.

Source Notes: **Jane W. Washburn.** Interviewed by Jennie Valyer, December 3, 2003, for the Hudson Falls HS World War II Living History Project. South Glens Falls, NY. Deposited at NYS Military Museum.

Source Notes: **Elaine Curren Sommo.** Interviewed by Jared Hunt, December 10, 2003, for the Hudson Falls HS World War II Living History Project. Hudson Falls, NY. Deposited at NYS Military Museum.

Source Notes: **Spencer Kulani.** Interviewed by Victor Ikeda, January 4, 2006, for the Hudson Falls HS World War II Living History Project. Hudson Falls, NY. Deposited at NYS Military Museum.

Source Notes: **Kathryn Goodman Frentzos.** Interviewed by Megan Seeley, January 11, 2010; Abigail George, December 6, 2010; and Alexandria Cartier, December 17, 2011. Queensbury, NY. Hudson Falls HS World War II Living History Project. Deposited at NYS Military Museum.

Source Notes: **Katherine G. Denegar.** Interviewed by Michael Russert and Wayne Clarke, October 3, 2003. Latham, NY. Deposited at NYS Military Museum.

Source Notes: **Lillian Lorraine Yonally.** Interviewed by Wayne Clarke, August 27, 2009, Colonie, NY. Deposited at NYS Military Museum.

Source Notes: **Rose Landsman Miller.** Interviewed by Wayne Clarke, November 5, 2009, Pine Plains, NY. Deposited at NYS Military Museum.

Source Notes: **Margaret Doris Alund Lear.** Interviewed by Michael Russert and Wayne Clarke, December 16, 2002. Saratoga Springs, NY. Deposited at NYS Military Museum.

Source Notes: **Helen Marcil Brennan.** Interviewed by Wayne Clarke, September 21, 2012. Troy, NY. Deposited at NYS Military Museum.

Source Notes: **Rose Landsman Miller.** Interviewed by Wayne Clarke, November 5, 2009, Pine Plains, NY. Deposited at NYS Military Museum.

Source Notes: **Kathleen Mary Davie.** Interviewed by Megan Shuler, January 5, 2006, for the Hudson Falls HS World War II Living History Project. Hudson Falls, NY. Deposited at NYS Military Museum.

Source Notes: **Joyce Griffin.** Interviewed by Sara Weiskotten, December 20, 2004, for the Hudson Falls HS World War II Living History Project. Hudson Falls, NY. Deposited at NYS Military Museum.

Source Notes: **Joan Hoffman.** Interviewed by Adam Armstrong, December 8, 2007, for the Hudson Falls HS World War II Living History Project. Hudson Falls, NY. Deposited at NYS Military Museum.

Source Notes: **Halina Roman.** Interviewed by Eric Roman, December 15, 2007, for the Hudson Falls HS World War II Living History Project. Erie, PA. Deposited at NYS Military Museum.

Source Notes: **Eva Koenig.** Interviewed by Lauren Ellmers, November 25, 2006, for the Hudson Falls HS World War II Living History Project. Hudson Falls, NY. Deposited at NYS Military Museum.

Source Notes: **Lily Muller.** Interviewed by Jackie Goodale, December 19, 2007, for the Hudson Falls HS World War II Living History Project. Hudson Falls, NY. Deposited at NYS Military Museum.

---

[1] Terkel, Studs. *"The Good War": An Oral History of World War II* (New York: Pantheon, 1984). Location 2239.

[2] *World War II and the American Home Front: A National Historic Landmarks Theme Study.* National Park Service, U.S. Department of the Interior. October, 2007. Location 4098.

[3] *World War II and the American Home Front: A National Historic Landmarks Theme Study.* National Park Service, U.S. Department of the Interior. October, 2007. Location 1985.

[4] *World War II and the American Home Front: A National Historic Landmarks Theme Study.* National Park Service, U.S. Department of the Interior. October, 2007. 10.

[5] *B-24 Liberator Assembly Line at Ford Willow Run Bomber Plant, 1944.* The Henry Ford, 2023. www.thehenryford.org/collections-and-research/digital-collections/artifact/369253/

[6] Rhodes, Richard. *The Making of the Atomic Bomb.* New York: Simon & Schuster, 1986.

[7] Recollection of Leona Gustafson. *World War II and the American Home Front: A National Historic Landmarks Theme Study.* National Park Service, U.S. Department of the Interior. October, 2007. Location 6604.

[8] Leonard, Chris. *World War II at 75: General Electric's key contributions.* The Schenectady Daily Gazette, July 27, 2020. dailygazette.com/2020/07/27/world-war-ii-at-75-general-electric-s-key-contributions

[9] Kannenberg, Lisa. *The Impact of the Cold War on Women's Activism: The UE Experience. Labor History*, 1993. www.ueunion.org/ue-news/2010/helen-quirini-1920-2010-fighter-for-equality-and-justice

[10] *their fellow women classmates would often pool their money and ship the body home-* Lillian Yonally obituary, *Albany Times Union*, Jan. 6, 2022.

[11] Source: *Women with Wings: The 75-Year-Legacy of the WASP.* National Air and Space Museum, Aug. 5, 2018. https://airandspace.si.edu/stories/editorial/women-wings-75-year-legacy-wasp

[12] Source: *The Army Nurse Corps in World War II.* U.S. Army Center of Military History, p. 26.

[13] Source: *The Army Nurse Corps in World War II.* U.S. Army Center of Military History, p. 15.

[14] *Polish Refugees in Iran During World War II.* Holocaust Encyclopedia, United States Holocaust Memorial Museum. encyclopedia.ushmm.org/content/en/article/polish-refugees-in-iran-during-world-war-ii

[15] Muller, Lily. Unpublished Memoir.

[16] Holocaust Encyclopedia. United States Holocaust Memorial Museum. *Warsaw Ghetto.* www.ushmm.org/wlc/en/article.php?ModuleId=10005069